Fatherland or Mother Earth?

Fatherland or Mother Earth?
Essays on the National Question

Michael Löwy

Pluto  Press

LONDON · STERLING, VIRGINIA
with

The International Institute for Research and Education (IIRE)

First published 1998 by Pluto Press
345 Archway Road, London N6 5AA
and 22883 Quicksilver Drive, Sterling, VA 21066–2012, USA

English translations copyright © Michael Löwy and IIRE 1998

The right of Michael Löwy to be identified as the author of this work
has been asserted by him in accordance with the Copyright, Designs
and Patents Act 1988.

British Library Cataloguing-in-Publication Data
A catalogue record for this book is available from the British Library
ISBN 0 7453 1348 5 hbk

IIRE Notebook for Study and Research no. 27–28

Library of Congress Cataloging in Publication Data
A catalog record for this book is available from the Library of Congress

Designed and produced for Pluto Press by
Chase Production Services, Chadlington, OX7 3LN
Typeset from disk by Gawcott Typesetting Services
Printed in the EC by Athenaeum Press, Gateshead

Contents

IIRE Notebooks for Study and Research

Thousands, even millions, of social activists in trade unions, non-governmental organisations (NGOs), ecological movements, and students' and women's organisations are wrestling with questions about a changing, globalising world. What ended and what began in history when the Berlin Wall fell? What realistic models can we put forward now in opposition to the reigning neo-liberalism? How can we resist neo-liberalism's lurking counterparts: nationalism, racism, fundamentalism, communalism?

The International Institute for Research and Education shares these grassroots activists' values: their conviction that societies can and must be changed, democratically, from below, by those who suffer from injustice, on the basis of wide-ranging international solidarity. We exist to help progressives pose the questions and find the answers that they need.

Since 1982 we have welcomed hundreds of participants from over 40 countries to our courses and seminars. Our Ernest Mandel Study Centre, opened in 1995, hosts lectures and conferences on economic and social issues of the post-Cold War world. We have built a network of Fellows who help with these tasks. Our Amsterdam headquarters and library are a resource for researchers and for gatherings of socially-minded non-profit groups.

Since 1986 the results of our work – on economic globalisation, twentieth-century history, ecology, feminism, ethnicity, racism, radical movement strategy and other topics – have been made available to a larger public through our monograph series, the Notebooks for Study and Research. The series is now published in English in book format by Pluto Press. Past Notebooks have also been published in other languages, including Arabic, Dutch, French, German, Japanese, Korean, Portuguese, Russian, Spanish, Swedish and Turkish. Back issues of the 20 pre-Pluto Press Notebooks are still available directly from the IIRE.

For information please write to us: IIRE, Postbus 53290, 1007 RG Amsterdam, Netherlands; email: iire@antenna.nl. Donations to support our work are tax-deductible in several European countries as well as in the US.

Foreword

The link between national and social emancipation has been one of the IIRE Notebooks for Study and Research's concerns from our inception. Over the years different titles have addressed such aspects of the problem as national resistance to Western domination in China and Latin America (NSRs 2, 3 and 6); Catalan and Basque movements (NSRs 13 and 16); and the failure of the multi-national experiment in Yugoslavia (NSR 19/20). Yet strangely enough, until now IIRE Fellow Michael Löwy has never had an opportunity to develop his analyses of nationalism and internationalism in a Notebook.

Despite all his other work as a prolific writer and as director of research in sociology for France's National Centre for Scientific Research, Löwy has been one of the IIRE's closest collaborators. He has written a Notebook for us entitled *Marxism and Liberation Theology* (NSR 10), edited our anthology *Populism in Latin America* (NSR 6) and allowed us to publish a French version of his book *The Politics of Combined and Uneven Development*. He has also been writing extensively on 'the national question' for over 20 years. But not for us.

Despite our earlier neglect of his writings on this subject, we now have the good fortune to publish in English the most complete work he has ever devoted to it (which has been, or is being, also published in French, German, Greek, Portuguese and Spanish). *Fatherland or Mother Earth?* brings together years of reflection on various Marxist thinkers. At the same time it integrates such recent developments as economic globalisation; the formation or reinforcement of supranational economic units like the European Union, NAFTA and MERCOSUR; the wave of national conflicts in the former Soviet bloc; and outbreaks of ethnic violence in many parts of the Third World. Finally, it pleads for a new and original synthesis (new even for Löwy himself) between Lenin's programme of national self-determination and Otto Bauer's programme of national-cultural autonomy.

For the opportunity to publish this book, we gratefully acknowledge those who have granted us permission to reprint parts of it that first appeared elsewhere (often in different form). Chapter 1, 'Marx and Engels Cosmopolites', was first published in *Critique* no. 14, 1981. Chapter 2 (co-authored with Enzo Traverso) appeared originally under the title 'The Marxist approach to the national question' in *Science and Society* vol. 54, no. 2, summer 1990. Chapter 3, first published in French in 1974 as part of Löwy's introduction to a French anthology of 'classical' Marxist texts on the national question edited in collaboration with his friends Georges Haupt and Claudie Weill, appeared first in English translation as part of the article 'Marxists and the national question' in *New Left Review* no. 96, April 1976. Chapter 4 was previously published in French in *Le Messager Européen* in 1993. Chapters 5, 6 and 7, finally, were written in 1989 and 1993 for the English journal *Socialist Register,* at the request of its editor, Ralph Miliband. We particularly appreciate current *Socialist Register* editor Leo Panitch's permission to borrow the title originally used for Chapters 5 and 7, 'Fatherland or Mother Earth?'.

Introduction

One of the most surprising aspects of this *fin-de-siècle* is the fantastic rise of nationalism, under various guises, both in the 'North' and the 'South'. Since this coincided, historically, with the demise of so-called 'really existing socialism', it was easy to jump to the conclusion that internationalism and socialism are 'dead' and that Marxism, unable to cope with the national movements, has become obsolete.

In fact this is not a new argument. It has been frequently put forward, by various sorts of commentators, that the Marxist tradition has ignored the national question (a so-called 'black hole' in the theory) or that national movements cannot be explained from a Marxist viewpoint. It cannot be denied that Marxists have often underestimated the importance of national problems. But it is also true, in my view, that one can find, in the Marxist literature, some very significant and rich contributions in this area. This does not mean, of course, that there are not also lacunae, contradictions, mistakes and hasty judgements.

The essays collected in this volume are of two kinds: first, comments on some important aspects of Marxist theory in relation to the national question; and second, an attempt to analyse, from a Marxist perspective, some contemporary forms of nationalism and internationalism. The three central contentions of the volume are the following: 1. internationalism is the core of the Marxian socialist tradition and it is more relevant now than ever; 2. the distinction between 'oppressor' and 'oppressed' nations and the idea of national/cultural autonomy, far from being contradictory, are complementary tools for understanding and solving national conflicts; 3. while nationalism is on the rise everywhere, there are also signs of the emergence of a new internationalism.

The first chapter, 'Marx and Engels Cosmopolites', deals with the philosophical background to Marxian internationalism, as the expression of a revolutionary humanist viewpoint. It seems to me important to begin this collection on the national question with a piece discussing the meaning of internationalism, because this is the strategic and methodological starting point for the Marxist approach. Moreover, today, in a world confronted with capitalist globalisation, the Marxian revolutionary kind of cosmopolitanism appears as an adequate alternative.

The second chapter examines some of the shortcomings of Marx and Engels's writings on the national question, while rejecting the view (presented by the historian Ephraim Nimni) that their conception is basically evolutionist and Eurocentric. I wrote this short polemical piece with my friend Enzo Traverso, a Marxist historian who has published several remarkable pieces on the national question (including *The Marxists and the Jewish Question*). As we see in the other chapters, Marx and Engels's incomplete theory of nationalities could be developed in a dogmatic, Eurocentric and evolutionist way (as Stalin did) or in an emancipatory and dialectical way (as Lenin, Bauer and others did).

The key issue in the third chapter is Lenin's classical distinction between oppressor and oppressed nations – still a relevant concept, even if one takes into account the various cases of rapid transformation of oppressed into oppressor – and his conception of the right to self-emancipation.

The Leninist tradition (including myself in earlier writings) has been rather harsh with the Austro-Marxist proposal for cultural autonomy. I feel that a more balanced assessment of Otto Bauer is needed, which I try to sketch in Chapter 4. As Georges Haupt observed in an essay on Bauer, his seminal book on the national question 'was a model of concrete research and of theoretical generalisation ... and remains the major reference work, indispensable for any historical and theoretical study of the national question'.[1]

Moreover one should acknowledge that Bauer was and remained strongly committed to socialist internationalism. In the new preface he wrote in 1924 for his book, he concludes with the following call: 'The duty of the International can and should be, not to abolish national particularities, but to promote international unity in national diversity'. Lenin himself, although quite critical of some of Bauer's political propositions, insisted that 'Otto Bauer ... argues quite correctly on a large number of most important questions'. For example, Lenin mentions Bauer's conviction that only the abolition of capitalism and the introduction of socialism will make it possible to abolish national oppression.[2]

One can understand Lenin's strong reservations about Bauer's (and the Jewish Bund's) programme for separate national schools, which he compares to the system of school segregation in the Southern US. However, Lenin's general rejection of Bauer's perspective of national/cultural autonomy is questionable. As Enzo Traverso insightfully observed in his book on the Marxists and the Jewish question, by confronting minority populations with a choice between assimilation and self-determination, the Bolshevik policy could not give a satis- factory answer to the problems of the extra-territorial nations, which rejected the first solution but did not dispose of the objective conditions necessary for the second.[3]

In fact, the Bolshevik government, at least during the first years of Soviet power, implemented, in relation to the Jewish and other national minorities, a policy very much inspired by the ideas of national/cultural autonomy proposed by Bauer and by the Bund: for instance, in developing Yiddish schools, theatres, publishing houses, libraries, etc.

In conclusion, it seems to me that, in the light of historical experience – including the recent catastrophic forms of decom- position of multi-national states (the USSR and Yugoslavia) – territorial self-determination and national/cultural autonomy should be considered complementary rather than mutually exclusive.

Towards a New Internationalism

The last chapters relate to the contemporary rise of nationalism and possibilities for the rise of a new internationalism. These essays are an attempt to use essential Marxist categories, as presented in the previous historical essays, to understand current developments related to the national question in Europe and the world, *and* to propose socialist, democratic and emancipatory alternatives to national exclusivism, chauvinism and xenophobia.

Rereading Chapter 5, first written in 1989, today, I have to acknowledge at least one obvious shortcoming: I did *not* foresee the explosive wave of internal national conflicts among the various communities of the ex-socialist bloc. I mentioned only the *emancipatory* dimension of movements against national oppression in the post-capitalist societies, neglecting the possibility that they could also become regressive, discriminatory (against their own minorities) and expansionist. I hope that Chapter 6, written a few years later, strikes a better balance.

All these chapters proclaim their hope for the rise of a new internationalism. This standpoint does not imply any kind of naïve optimism or short-term illusions. In the present conjuncture and the near future this is not very likely to happen. It means rather that one puts a *wager* (in the sense that Lucien Goldmann refers to socialism as a secular wager analogous to Pascal's *pari*) on the possibility of a different future, where universal human solidarity will again become a powerful force in the political struggle.

Since I wrote these essays an important event has taken place, illustrating the dialectics between national emancipation and internationalism. The Zapatista movement in Chiapas, Mexico, convened an 'Intercontinental Conference against Neoliberalism and for Humanity' in the summer of 1996. When it appeared in the insurrection of January 1994, the EZLN – Zapatista Army of National Liberation – raised the demand of national/cultural autonomy for indigenous communities and of Mexican national sovereignty against the US-imposed free-trade agreement (NAFTA). But in 1996 the Zapatistas, for the first time in Latin America, called for an internationalist meeting, not on a continental or Third World level, but on a truly planetary scale. The 'Intergalactic' gathering in Chiapas in July 1996 was attended by intellectuals, left activists, trade unionists, and indigenous, peasant, feminist and other social activists from Canada to Brazil, from Japan to Italy, and from France to South Africa. There is room for hope ... .

CHAPTER 1

Marx and Engels Cosmopolites

How did Marx and Engels conceive the place of nations in future communist society? We know the authors of the *Communist Manifesto* were somewhat reserved towards attempts to play *Zukunftmusik* and examine too closely the horizons of the future. This does not prevent us finding in a series of their early writings (between 1845 and 1848) a number of statements on the subject of the nation in a communist society, some of which exerted an influence on the Russian workers movement and, particularly, on Lenin's thinking.

There are notably some paragraphs in the *Manifesto* which for more than a century have invited the most contradictory interpretations and the bitterest polemics:

> The Communists are further reproached with desiring to abolish countries and nationality. The working men have no country. We cannot take from them what they have not got. Since the proletariat must first of all acquire political supremacy, must rise to be the leading class of the nation, must constitute itself the nation, it is so far, itself national, though not in the bourgeois sense of the word. National differences (*Absonderungen*) and antagonisms between peoples are daily more and more vanishing, owing to the development of the bourgeoisie, to freedom of commerce, to the world market, to uniformity in the mode of production and in the conditions of life corresponding thereto.
>
> The supremacy (*Herrschaft*) of the proletariat will cause them to vanish still faster. United action, of the leading civilised countries at least, is one of the first conditions for the emancipation of the proletariat.
>
> In proportion as the exploitation of one individual by another is put an end to, the exploitation of one nation by another will also be put an end to. In proportion as the

antagonism between classes within the nation vanishes, the hostility of one nation to another will come to an end.[1]

In this article, what interests us most is the *disappearance of national differences and antagonisms.* A preliminary observation is called for. In the eyes of Marx and Engels, what is involved is a process already very much engaged in by the bourgeoisie itself which the proletariat will above all have to complete and perfect. It is a thesis stemming from a surprising *free-trade optimism* and from a somewhat 'economist' procedure, inasmuch as 'uniformity in the mode of production and in the conditions of life corresponding thereto' is supposed to lead by itself to the decline in national conflicts. However, it must be added that in other contemporary writings, Engels as well as Marx insists on the impossibility of a solution to national contradictions within the framework of the capitalist mode of production. For example, in his report on the internationalist meeting in London in September 1845, Engels wrote:

> The fantasies about a European Republic, perpetual peace under political organisation, have become just as ridiculous as the phrases about uniting the nations under the aegis of universal free trade ... The bourgeoisie in each country has its own special interests, and ... can never transcend nationality ... [2]

A passage in *The German Ideology* helps to clear up the contradictions for us: it is not the bourgeoisie as such, but *large-scale industry* which eliminates national barriers by the creation of a new class, radically international, *the proletariat*: ' ... [W]hile the bourgeoisie of each nation still retained separate national interests, large-scale industry created a class which in all nations has the same interest and for which nationality is already dead ... '[3]

This clearly recalls the well-known formula, 'The proletariat has no country', which is not only ironic whimsy but which corresponds to a total conception of Marx and Engels, namely: (a) *the national state* belongs not to the proletariat but to the bourgeoisie;[4] (b) the material, economic, social and political conditions of the proletariat are the same in all industrial countries. As Marx wrote in a fiercely ironical passage in his notes on the German economist, Friedrich List (recently discovered in the archives by Marx's grandson, Marcel-Charles Longuet):

> The nationality of the worker is neither French, nor English, nor German, it is *labour, free slavery, self-huckstering (Selbstverschacherung)*. His government is neither French, nor English, nor German, it is *capital*. His native air is neither French, nor German, nor English, it is *factory air*. The land belonging to him is neither French, nor English, nor German, it lies a few feet *below the ground*.[5]

It follows that, for Marx and Engels, only the proletariat, as a universal class which is no longer national and which has common world-historical interests, can lead to the establishment of a universal society where national differences will be overcome (we shall see later the precise meaning of the term 'national differences'). In his report on the internationalist meeting in London (1845), Engels is to develop this theme in an explicit, radical and forceful way:

> The proletarians in all countries have one and the same interest, one and the same enemy, and one and the same struggle. The great mass of proletarians are by their very nature, free from national prejudices and their entire disposition (*Bildung*) and movement is essentially humanitarian (*humanitarisch*), anti-national ... Only the awakening proletariat can bring about fraternisation between the different nations'.[6]

In some of Engel's writings, this humanitarian and 'anti-national' conception was called *cosmopolitanism*. For example, in the same 1845 report, Engels hails a meeting held in London the previous year (10 August) in the following words: 'Already in this festival of August 10th there had been expressed principles that were both communist and cosmopolitic'; and the meeting of September 1845, whose spirit of international fraternity the article describes with enthusiasm, is called 'a cosmopolitan festival'.[7] Obviously,

Engels takes good care to distinguish this communist cosmopolitanism from 'the hypocritical, private-egotistical cosmopolitanism of free trade',[8] and from the pseudo-cosmopolitanism of a 'socialist patriot' like Louis Blanc. In a speech given in Dijon in December 1847, Louis Blanc had put forward the idea that France was the cosmopolitan nation *par excellence* and that to work for the future of France was identical with working for the future of humanity. In a polemical article of 30 December 1847, Engels comments ironically on this very individual conception of cosmopolitanism:

> '*A Frenchman is necessarily a cosmopolite,*' says M. Blanc. Yes, in a world ruled over only by French influence, French manners, fashions, ideas, politics. In a world in which every nation has adopted the characteristics of French nationality. But that is exactly what the democrats of other nations will not accept. Quite ready to give up the harshness of their own nationality, they expect the same from the French. They will not be satisfied in the assertion on the part of the French that they are cosmopolites by the mere fact that they *are* French, an assurance which amounts to the demand urged on all others to *become* French.[9]

Engel's article ends with the following remark which once again shows the *positive* meaning he gives to the word 'cosmopolitanism': 'If we were to apply the measure of M. Blanc, the Germans would be the true cosmopolites. However, the German democrats are far from having any such pretensions'.[10] In a footnote, the East German editors (of the Marx-Engels *Werke*) point out: 'The words "cosmopolitism" and "cosmopolite" are here used by Engels not in the sense of Louis Blanc's speech or in the sense of *bourgeois* cosmopolitism criticised by this article, but rather in the proper meaning of the words, "universally humanitarian" and "free of national prejudices".' In addition, in the glossary of foreign terms at the end of the volume, we find the following translation: 'Cosmopolite: (here) international'.[11] In other words, there is no doubt that Engels considered himself to be a 'communist cosmopolite' and that 'cosmopolitanism' in his political dictionary was a word analogous to internationalism.

The word continued to be so used by Engels even much later: for example, in a letter of September 1874 to F.A. Sorge he refers in the following words to the period of the founding of the First International: 'It was the moment when the common, cosmopolitan interests of the proletariat could be put in the foreground'.[12]

It is well known that at the time of the great Stalinist trials of 1949–52 in Eastern Europe a huge campaign of denunciation of 'cosmopolitanism' was developed inside the Communist movement. In the course of the trials (notably of Slansky and his friends) the accusation of 'cosmopolitanism', closely linked to that of 'Zionism' and 'Trotskyism', was launched by the prosecutor, in particular against defendants of Jewish origin.[13] Within the framework of this campaign, various attempts were made by intellectuals and theoreticians of the Communist movement in Western Europe to mobilise the writings of Marx and Engels in merciless struggle against cosmopolitanism. One of the most typical examples of these attempts is *Réalité de la Nation: L'attrape-nigaud du cosmopolitisme,* a work by Georges Cogniot.[14]

For his anti-cosmopolitan proof, Cogniot uses a passage from *The German Ideology* in which Marx criticises the German 'true socialists'. According to Marx, the writings of this current show 'the narrowly national outlook which underlies the alleged universalism and cosmopolitanism of the Germans'.[15] To our mind, the text clearly shows that: (a) for Marx, cosmopolitanism is assimilated to universalism and both are opposed to narrow nationalism; and (b) for him, the Germans *allege* they are cosmopolites, but are not so, given their nationalist mentality. But, according to Cogniot, the meaning of the passage is as follows: 'Marx used the example of these pseudo-socialists to show that nationalism and cosmopolitanism go hand-in-hand ... '[16]

In addition, Cogniot quotes in support of his thesis the above passage from Engels's article against Louis Blanc. However, he suppresses a clause which seems to upset his proof, namely, that in which Engels explains that the democrats of all nations are 'quite ready to give up the harshness of their own nationality'. And further: while the editors of the *Marx-Engels Werke* recognise that Engels counterposes genuine cosmopolitanism ('in the proper sense of the word') to the *pseudo-cosmopolitanism* of Louis Blanc, Cogniot presents Engels's position as a rejection of cosmopolitanism *in principle*.

Finally: Cogniot relies on Engels' criticism of the 'hypocritical cosmopolitanism of free trade' in the 1845 report for proof of the anti-cosmopolitanism of its author, while keeping silent on the fact that in this article, Engels explicitly extols communist cosmopolitanism (which he distinguishes, clearly, from that of bourgeois free trade). Cogniot's conclusion is clear and sharp: 'Such indications from Marx and Engels have the value of a principle. They are sufficient to prove that Marxism has nothing in common with cosmopolitanism ... '[17] The least one can say is that this conclusion corresponds rather more to certain political requirements of the year 1950 than to a rigorous analysis of the texts of Marx and Engels of 1845–48. In reality, the idea of a *cosmopolis, a universal city* going beyond national frontiers, is to be found at the heart of the reflections of Marx and Engels on the national question in this period. They were not concerned as the philosophers of ancient Greece had been with a purely moral aspiration but with a political project on a world-historical scale that would result from revolutionary upheaval. In *The German Ideology,* Marx emphasises that it is only through a communist revolution that history becomes wholly 'world history' (*Weltgeschichte*). It is only such a revolution which will

> liberate the separate individuals from the various national and local barriers, bring them into practical connection with the production (including intellectual production) of the whole world and make it possible for them to acquire the capacity to enjoy this all-sided production of the whole earth (the creation of man).[18]

From this standpoint, the nation appears as a stage in the historical development of humanity which cannot accede to a higher stage of universality:

> What the nations have done as nations, they have done for human society; their whole value consists only in the fact that each single nation has accomplished for the benefit of

other nations one of the main historical aspects (one of the main determinations) in the framework of which mankind has accomplished its development, and therefore after industry in England, politics in France and philosophy in Germany have been developed, they have been developed for the world, and their world-historical significance, as also that of these nations, has thereby come to an end.[19]

It is in the light of these considerations that we must interpret the little phrase in the *Manifesto* on the abolition of national differences and antagonisms. In addition, we should note that this phrase corresponds not only to the political and teleological positions of Marx and Engels but also to the tendencies expressed by the communist currents of the workers movement of the time. In his classical work on the national question, the Austro-Marxist Otto Bauer was to speak of the 'simple cosmopolitanism' of the first early years of the proletarian movement, a cosmopolitanism flowing from 'the idea of *Humanity*'.[20] In fact, the conceptions developed in the *Manifesto* on the future of nations come very close to the doctrine of the Communist League (the workers organisation which had asked Engels to edit the text). The first draft of the 'Communist Profession of Faith' approved by the Congress of the League in June 1847 (a draft drawn up jointly by Engels and the worker leaders of the League) contains the following formulation which is even more radical than that of the *Manifesto*:

Question 21: Will Nationalities continue to exist under communism?

Answer: The nationalities of the peoples who join according to the principle of communism will be just as much compelled by this union to merge with one another and thereby supersede themselves as the various differences between estates and classes disappear through the superseding of their basis – private property.[21]

It is of interest to note that in *The Principles of Communism* which Engels was to draw up in October 1847 (a text which repeats in part the June version but which makes editorial changes in several chapters) there is the following note which suggests approval of the passage on nationalities in the first draft: '22: What will be the attitude of the communist organisation towards existing nationalities?. Answer: No change.'[22]

The definitive version in the *Manifesto* is *more moderate*: it is only a matter of abolishing the national conflicts and *Absonderungen*. Clearly, everything depends on how we translate this word, which can be rendered as 'differences', 'separation' or 'isolation'.

Several interpretations, both of the *Manifesto* and of the other writings of Marx and Engels on this subject during the years 1845–48, have been put forward, by Marxists, Marxoids and Marxologists of various tendencies. Some are rather 'minimalist', like Solomon Bloom in his well-known work on the national question in Marx. According to Bloom:

> *The Manifesto* is a cryptic and epigrammatic document and therefore easily misread. What the authors foresaw was not the complete disappearance of all national distinctions whatever, but specifically the abolition of sharp economic and political differences, economic isolation, invidious distinctions, political rivalries, wars, and exploitation of one nation by another.[23]

This interpretation is not unlikely but it leaves out the radicalism of the writings of Marx and Engels from 1845 to 1848 and the perspective of the universal city which inspired them. Moreover, it offers no proof at the textual level that the term 'national differences' refers only to economic and social differences.

At the other extreme, some authors, such as Bertell Ollman, develop a rather 'maximalist' reading of Marx and Engel's remarks on the future of the nation. According to Ollman, in Marx's vision of communism:

> The divisions we are accustomed to seeing in the human species along lines of nation, race, religion, geographical section (town dwellers and country dwellers), occupation, class, and family have all ceased to exist. They are replaced

by new and as yet unnamed divisions more in keeping with the character of the people and life of the period.[24]

Ollman's merit is that he insists on the universal, world-human, supranational dimensions of the Marxian communist society. Moreover, he is one of the few authors to describe Marx's problematic as 'cosmopolitic', while at the same time showing that this society is in no way conceived by the authors of the *Manifesto* as being homogeneous, uniform or indivisible. But his interpretation goes too far, notably when he writes, in connection with a remark in *The German Ideology* about language being submitted 'to the perfect control of individuals':

> I interpret this to mean that one language will replace the thousands now in existence (whatever limited cultural role many languages may continue to play), and that it will be specially adapted to permit clear expression to the extraordinary experiences, understanding, and feelings of the people of this time.[25]

However this interpretation does not at all flow from Marx's own remark in *The German Ideology,* which speaks simply of the *control* by individuals over language, and in no way allows the meaning that national languages are fated to disappear. On the contrary, in the phrase which immediately follows, Marx is ironical about the 'Association' preached by Max Stirner in which only one language will be spoken: 'language as such will be spoken, holy language, the language of the holy – Hebrew, and indeed the Aramaic dialect'.[26] In reality there are very few references in Marx and Engels to the national question from the *cultural* standpoint: in a passage in *The German Ideology* Marx emphasises that: 'With a communist organisation of society there disappears the subordination of the artist to local and national narrowness',[27] but that does not allow us to draw general conclusions about the future of national cultures, as Ollman tries to do.[28]

A third interpretation, which seems to me the most likely, is that put forward by Roman Rosdolsky in a short note published in 1965: what Engels meant by 'abolition' (or even 'annihilation') of nationality is certainly not the 'abolition' of existing ethnic and linguistic communities (which would have been absurd) but of the *political* delimitation of peoples. In a society in which (in the words of *The Manifesto*) 'the public power will lose its political character' and *the State as such will wither away,* there can be no room for separate 'national States'.[29]

It is agreed that, as Marx emphasised in the *Manifesto,* the proletariat must first seize power within the framework of a national state, but this separate proletarian national state *'will be only a transitional stage towards the future classless and Stateless society,* since the construction of such a society is possible only on the international scale'.[30]

To sum up. Throughout the years 1845–48, in the writings of Marx and Engels there is a cosmopolitan/internationalist (the words are roughly interchangeable in the period) projection of a *world city,* a universal *Gemeinschaft,* in which not only national anatagonisms and conflicts will disappear but also *the economic, social and political* (but not cultural) *differences* between nations. This perspective of a *world without frontiers* is closely linked to their entire world-view, particularly: 1. their *humanitarian* problematic, that is, their reference to humanity as the ultimate framework of reflection and political praxis; 2. their vision of communism as a necessarily 'world-historical' system; 3. their thesis of the withering away of the state in the classless society of the future; and 4. their conception of the proletariat as a universal supranational class because of its material condition and objective interests.

It seems that after the 1848 revolution, during which the national question revealed itself to Marx and Engels in all its virulence and complexity, the two authors of the *Communist Manifesto* abandoned the cosmopolitan problematic of their early writings while retaining its internationalism, particularly the *present* political dimension. For example, in the *Critique of the Gotha Programme* (1875), Marx severely attacks the Lassalleans for having 'conceived the labour movement from the narrowest standpoint', and he counterposes to the slogan put forward by the *Gotha Programme,* 'the international brotherhood of the nations', that of 'the international brotherhood of the working classes in the joint struggle against the ruling classes and their governments';[31] but he does not put forward any perspective for the future by himself posing the question of the national state or 'national differences' at any level at all.

Why this silence? From tactical prudence, from political realism or from the conviction (acquired through the years) that the fact of the nation was more tenacious than anticipated? Unless it was from the fear that the cosmopolitan idea would be used as a pretext for a 'leading state' to absorb other nations within itself. In a letter to Engels of 20 June 1866, Marx reports on a meeting of the Council of the First International:

> The representatives (non-workers) of Young France came out with the announcement that all nationalities and even nations were 'antiquated prejudices'. Proudhonised Stirnerism. Everything to be dissolved into little 'groups' or 'communes' which will in their turn form an 'association', but no State. And indeed this 'individualisation' of mankind and the corresponding 'mutualism' are to proceed while history comes to a stop in all other countries and the whole world waits until the French are ripe for a social revolution. They will then perform the experiment before our eyes, and the rest of the world, overcome by the force of their example, will do the same.

> ... The English laughed very much when I began my speech by saying that our friend Lafargue and those who with him had done away with nationalities, had spoken 'French' to us, i.e. a language which nine-tenths of the audience did not understand. I also suggested that by the negation of nationalities he appeared, quite unconsciously, to understand their *absorption* into the model French nation.[32]

Marx feared that the cosmopolitan ideal might serve the claims to hegemony by a 'model nation'. He could not have foreseen that almost a century later (1949–52), by an irony of history, in Eastern Europe it was, among other things, in the name of 'the struggle against cosmopolitanism' that the partisans of the leading state and of 'socialism in one country' would exterminate their opponents, for the most part old-timers of the International Brigade in Spain.

CHAPTER 2

Marx and Engels Eurocentrists?[1]

Most historians (Marxist or not) emphasise the incompleteness and limitations of Marx and Engels's writings on the national question. The critique of Engels's theory of nations 'without history' – formulated for the first time at the beginning of this century by Otto Bauer in his monumental *Die Nationalitätenfrage und die Sozialdemokratie* (1907) and developed in a more systematic and rigorous way by the Ukrainian Marxist historian Roman Rosdolsky after the Second World War – has became today a solid acquisition of contemporary Marxist literature on the national question. In general, Marxist historians are inclined to consider the national problem as one of the main gaps in Marx and Engels's theoretical elaboration. In particular, they have analysed the category of the 'non-historical peoples' (*geschichtlosen Völker*) as basically contradictory to the premisses of Marxism.

Ephraim Nimni, however, in a dissenting view, thinks that 'Marx and Engels have a coherent view of the national question, even if there is no single corpus of literature that directly presents their theories in an explicit way'.[2] In his opinion the coherence of this conception is based on three fundamental 'paradigms' of historical materialism: 1. a theory of evolution, that is, a vision of history 'as a progressive series of changes through universal and hierarchically defined stages'; 2. a deterministic theory which analyses – through a form of 'economic reductionism' – all social changes as the automatic result of the growth of the forces of production; and 3. a 'Eurocentric' world that would represent the necessary and inevitable consequence of the two previous 'theoretical parameters'. After this premiss, the reader might well think that this study is conceived as a critique of Marxism as a whole. At the end, however, one discovers that Ephraim Nimni considers himself to be a Marxist, and appeals to a historical materialism purged of the 'misleading heritage of European Marxism'.

We understand Nimni's good intentions, but we think his attitude is quite contradictory. If we were convinced that Marx's theory was founded on a form of evolutionism and economic determinism inevitably opening on a Eurocentric worldview, we should certainly be anti-Marxists. In reality, the premiss of Nimni's essay is a caricature of Marx's thought and would be more appropriate as a characterisation of the quite different materialist worldviews elaborated by Kautsky, Plekhanov and Bukharin. Some writings of Marx and Engels, first of all the *Communist Manifesto*, undoubtedly present aspects of an evolutionist or economic determinist tendency in their interpretation of history. However, it would be totally wrong to reduce the whole of Marx's thought to a view of society and history as the result of natural laws of development of productive forces or as a series of stages according to the European model. Some of Nimni's critical remarks are indeed relevant – for instance, when he observes that Marx and Engels did not understand those nationalist movements that were neither willing nor able to establish a national state. But too often his analysis is extremely one-sided, generalising from isolated phrases; sometimes it tends to become a caricature bearing little resemblance to Marx's ideas.

Some passages of the *Communist Manifesto* can be read as a true apology of the historical work of capitalism in destroying the feudal order and, in general, all archaic social formations. Marx and Engels assigned a 'revolutionary' character to capitalism outside the frontiers of Europe, in a period in which, within the continent, they considered the conditions ripe for a socialist revolution. In India, Britain supposedly on the one hand destroyed the old society and, on the other hand, laid down the foundations for modern social development through the industrialisation of the country. In 1853 Marx defined England, the leading force of this social change, as the 'unconscious tool of history'.[3] In the same vein, Engels approved the annexation of California by the US because, according to his explanation, 'the energetic Yankees' would be better than 'the lazy Mexicans' in assuring the economic growth of the region.[4] In 1848 Engels even welcomed – as Nimni stresses –

the French conquest of Algeria as 'a happy event for the progress of civilisation'.[5]

Obviously, it is important to criticise and condemn these statements, but it would be wrong and schematic to see only these passages. In reality, Marx and Engels often denounced the mystification, deeply rooted in the Eurocentric culture of their epoch and in imperialist ideology, that presents colonial conquests as 'civilising missions'. They saw capitalism as a system that 'turns every economic progress into a social calamity'.[6] They were fascinated by the spread of capitalism on a world scale, but at the same time they denounced the barbaric and violent way in which this process was accomplished. In respect to the British colonisation of India, Marx compared 'human progress' to 'that hideous, pagan idol, who would not drink the nectar but from the skulls of the slain'.[7] In 1857, in an article on Algeria written for the *American Encyclopaedia*, Engels denounced 'the horrors of lust and brutality' of the French 'barbarous system of warfare' against the 'Arab and Kabyle tribes, to whom independence is precious weal and hatred of foreign domination a principle dearer than life itself'.[8] In 1861, Marx described the European expedition to Mexico as 'one of the most monstrous enterprises ever chronicled in the annals of international history'.[9] This statement, and those in favour of the Chinese in the 'Opium Wars' with England, are not at all typical of Eurocentrism.

Similarly, the evolutionistic interpretation of Marx cannot be accepted, because it schematises and impoverishes the complexity and the richness of his thought. Nimni reduces it to a famous passage in *Capital* that became a dogma for the positivistic Marxism of the Second International: 'the country that is more developed industrially shows, to the less developed, the image of its own future'.[10] At the turn of the century, Kautskyan 'orthodoxy' closed Marx's theory into the iron cage of this evolutionistic interpretation. The thought of Marx was so much identified with social Darwinistic theories that the young Gramsci welcomed the Russian revolution of 1917 as a 'revolution against *Capital*'.[11]

However, this single passage does not at all represent Marx's theory in its totality. He never claimed to transpose mechanically to all countries the development stages of

Western Europe – primitive communism, slavery, feudalism, capitalism – and his writings on pre-capitalist societies are hypotheses for further research, rather than unquestionable conclusions. With respect to Russia, in 1881–82 Marx considered the possibility of a direct transition from the *obshchina* (the Russian peasant community) to communism, without going through all the 'terrible ups and downs' of capitalism, if a peasant revolution in Russia should fuse together with a socialist revolution in Europe. In a letter sent in 1877 to the Russian review *Otechestvenniye Zapiski*, Marx warned the readers against the danger of transforming his 'historical sketch of the genesis of capitalism in Western Europe into a historico-philosophic theory of the general path every people is fated to tread, whatever the historic circumstances in which it finds itself'. In 1881 he reaffirmed the same concept in a famous letter to Vera Zasulich, where he presented the traditional rural community as the 'fulcrum for social regeneration in Russia'.[12] The Russian Marxists, led by Plekhanov, to whom the idea of 'skipping' capitalism appeared as a populist heresy, scrupulously hid this letter (it was found and published by Riazanov in 1911). It is only one example of the anti-evolutionist currents in Marx's writings.

Marx and Engels formulated an *idea,* more than an accomplished *theory,* of the national question. This fact constituted a limitation of their theoretical elaboration, but at the same time it protected them against the danger of a too-rigid and normative definition, like those proposed by Kautsky (the nation as an economic-linguistic-territorial entity) or Stalin (the nation as an economic, territorial, linguistic, cultural and psychological community).[13] Both German revolutionaries lived in an epoch still marked by the formation of some national states in Europe (Germany, Italy, Poland, Hungary) and this fact necessarily influenced their view. We can deduce from their writings a concept of the nation as a *historical formation* linked to the rise of the capitalist mode of production and crystallised in a political superstructure – the national state[14] – but this concept was never developed in a systematic way. This incompleteness in their analysis of the national question is probably linked to their belief that they lived in an epoch dominated by bourgeois cosmopolitanism and by the advent, in the near

future, of a socialism transcending national conflicts. In a
work such as the *Communist Manifesto,* cosmopolitanism and
internationalism tend to fuse. There, the internationalisation
of the capitalist mode of production and the formation of the
world market are seen as a process which 'has given a
cosmopolitan (*kosmopolitisch*) character to production and
consumption in every country', establishing a 'universal interdependence of nations' and creating a 'world literature'. In
this ceaseless transformation of social life, capitalism has made
'the country dependent on the towns ... the barbarian and
semi-barbarian countries dependent on the civilised ones,
nations of peasants on nations of bourgeois, the East on the
West'.[15] This admiring account of the revolutionary function
of the capitalist mode of production, viewed as an economic
system that would increasingly unify the world materially and
'spiritually' and suppress the basis for national conflicts,
certainly led the authors of the *Manifesto* to neglect the importance of the national question. This underestimation, which
doubtless contains some elements of economic reductionism
and Eurocentrism, marked in particular the writings of Marx
and Engels in 1848–49.

It is true that the *Communist Manifesto* contains some
doubtful formulations. It is, however, inaccurate to write, as
Nimni does, that for Marx and Engels 'the nation will be abol-
ished by the advancing tide of history'. What they wrote is that
the supremacy of the proletariat will cause the disappearance of
'national delimitations (*Absonderungen*) and antagonisms
between peoples'. The most likely interpretation of this phrase
is in our opinion the one presented by Roman Rosdolsky in his
1965 essay: when Marx and Engels hoped that in a communist
society national antagonisms and delimitations will disappear,
they meant 'certainly not the "abolition" of existing ethnic and
linguistic communities' but of national antagonisms and
conflicts as well as economic, social and political (*but not
cultural*) differences between nations.[16]

The Irish example illuminates a different theoretical
approach to the national phenomenon that can be found in
Marx and Engels. The criterion that brought them to recognise Ireland as a historical nation was not *economic,* but essentially *political.* Their starting point was the understanding of

the Irish people's wish to become an independent nation. In Ireland, nationalism grew stronger in direct proportion to the process of *denationalisation* carried out by British imperialism. This process determined not only the economic spoliation of the island, but even a true linguistic assimilation of the Irish, who abandoned the Gaelic tongue in order to speak English. Engels wrote: 'After the cruelest repression, after every attempt at extermination, the Irish quickly raised themselves again, stronger than before; they even drew their main strength from the foreign garrison that was imposed upon them in order to oppress them.'[17]

In this case, the concept of nation was not defined according to *objective* criteria (economy, language, territory, etc.), but rather was founded on a *subjective* element: the will of the Irish to liberate themselves from British rule. This conception, in which it is difficult to find any signs of 'economic reductionism', instead emphasised the importance of national identity and interiority. In 1939 Trotsky adopted the same method, in a discussion with C.L.R. James about the Black question in America, arguing that 'on this matter an abstract criterion is not decisive, but the historical consciousness, the feelings and the impulses of a group are more important'.[18] In reality, the two main Marxist interpretations of the national phenomenon – on one hand, the economic and deterministic theory of Kautsky and Stalin and, on the other, the historical and cultural theory of Bauer and Trotsky – both issue from the classical Marxist approach, whose incompleteness and fluidity can be developed in either an evolutionistic or a dialectical way.

In his attempt to prove that Marx's views are not fragmentary and incomplete, but a systematic and coherent 'evolutionist' whole, Nimni argues that his (and Engels's) 'fundamental theoretical assumption' was that 'every national state' is 'indissolubly linked with the universalisation of the capitalist mode of production and the hegemony of the bourgeoisie'. This explains, according to him, Marx and Engels's 'firm advocacy of the right of self-determination to the Irish and Poles', and at the same time their harsh treatment of the 'southern Slavs'. Now, far from supporting Ireland because of 'bourgeois hegemony', Marx was very pleased that the hegemonic forces in the Irish national and agrarian struggle, the Fenians, were 'characterised by a socialist tendency (in a negative sense, directed against the appropriation of the soil)'.[19] Their reasons for supporting Poland, and not Serbian or Bohemian nationalism, were not economistic ('the universalisation of the capitalist economy') but exclusively political: the Polish national movement was anti-tsarist, while the others were considered by Marx to be manipulated by tsarism. In the case of the South Slavs, one can argue that his political attitude was wrong; one cannot prove that it was the logical outcome of a general 'evolutionist' and 'Eurocentric' view (by the way, why should Poland be more 'European' than, say, Bohemia?) and even less of the 'classical epistemology of Marxism'.

'Non-historical' Nations

With respect to the theory of 'non-historical nations', there is a basic contradiction in Nimni's argument. On the one hand, he writes that this theory is 'a clear effect' of the 'classical Marxist epistemology' with its 'universal processes of social transformation'. But two pages later he observes that this Hegelian conceptualisation is 'in direct opposition to a historical materialist conception of history'! He even considers it 'strange' to find such 'idealist speculations' echoed 'in the works of the founders of historical materialism'.[20] We entirely agree with this last thesis, but it is obviously incompatible with the first one.

The other problem is that Nimni insists on attributing to Marx the same views as Engels about the 'non-historical peoples', offering very little evidence for this. Let us examine his argument:

(a) It is 'unthinkable' that Marx and Engels 'would disagree over such a fundamental issue'. Well, this begs a question. There is nothing to show that Marx either agreed or disagreed with this theory (or did not care to take a stand): the fact is that *he did not use it in his writings*. It is therefore arbitrary to impute such views to him. Differences between Marx and Engels have been observed by Marxist philosophers and scholars on several issues without necessarily involving any explicit disagreement. There is no reason why this should be 'unthinkable' in relation to the national question.

(b) 'Marx also indulged in a derogatory denunciation of small and non-western European national communities.' He used 'abusive language' and was 'impatient and intolerant with ethnic minorities'. As examples, Nimni quotes some remarks about Spaniards, Mexicans and Chinese. Now, none of those nations is an 'ethnic minority' and none was considered as 'non-historic' by either Marx or Engels (each already had a state). And Spaniards are not – either geographically or historically – a 'small' or 'non-Western' nation!

Moreover, the quotation about China is taken completely out of context by Nimni. Far from being 'derogatory' towards China, this article projects that 'the next uprising of the people of Europe ... may depend more probably on what is now passing in the Celestial Empire – the very opposite of Europe – than any other political cause that now exists ... . It may safely be augured that the Chinese revolution will throw the spark into the overloaded mine of the present industrial system and cause the explosion of the long prepared general crisis, which, spreading abroad, will be closely followed by political revolutions in the Continent'.[21] Far from being 'Eurocentric', this prediction – alas, entirely wrong, as were many other wildly optimistic predictions of Marx and his followers – is surprisingly akin to the most extreme 'Third Worldism' of the 1960s.

True, Marx often refers to the Chinese nation as 'semibarbarian'. But writing about the Chinese war against English imperialism in 1858 he observes that this nation 'stood on the principle of morality' and was 'prompted by ethical motives' (the refusal to accept the opium trade), while 'the representative of overwhelming modern society fights for the privilege of buying in the cheapest and selling in the dearest market'.[22]

There is no doubt that one can find in both Marx and Engels all kinds of 'derogatory remarks' in reference to several nations; it is also true that their private correspondence contains some horrible expressions, like the infamous 'Jewish nigger' formula for Lassalle. But we do not believe that one can make a 'theory' out of all this, particularly if one considers that the great 'historical nations' (France, Germany, England) also receive their share of 'derogatory remarks'.

It is also true that there is in some of Marx's writings of the 1840s and 1850s a very negative assessment of the South Slav nations, but this was not organically linked to any general 'evolutionist, economicist and Eurocentric' philosophy. It was rather the ad hoc product of his obsessive fear of tsarist counter-revolution and of Panslavism as a tool of the tsar. As soon as the prospects of revolution in Russia began to materialise (after 1870), this negative assessment disappeared entirely from his writings.

Engels's approach to the so-called 'non-historical peoples' was very different. In his vocabulary this term designated the nations lacking the 'historical, geographical, political and industrial premises of independence and vitality'. Engels wrote:

> Peoples (*Völker*) which have never had a history of their own, which from the time when they achieved the first, most elementary stage of civilisation already come under foreign sway, or which were *forced* to attain the first stage of civilization only by means of a foreign yoke, are not viable (*haben keine Lebensfähigkeit*) and will never be able to achieve any kind of independence.[23]

Engels was referring to those nations that lived permanently under the political rule of a foreign state and that, in his opinion, were doomed to be assimilated by the socially and economically more advanced nations. Engels continued:

> There is no country in Europe which does not have in some corner or other one or several ruined fragments of peoples (*Völkerruinen*), the remnant of a former population that was suppressed and held in bondage by the nation which later became the main vehicle of historical development (*Trägerin der geschichtlichen Entwicklung*). These relics of a nation mercilessly trampled under foot in the course of history, as Hegel says these *residual fragments of peoples* (*Völkerabfalle*) always become fanatical standard-bearers of counter-revolution and remain so until their complete extirpation or loss of their national character (*gänzlichen Vertilgung oder Entnationalisierung*), just as their whole existence in general is itself a protest against a great historical revolution.[24]

This category included, according to Engels, the Gaels of Scotland, the Bretons, the Basques, the Yiddish-speaking Jews of Eastern Europe and, in particular, the Southern Slavs.

According to Engels, in 1848 the great European nations were on the side of revolution, while the Slavs (with the exception of the Poles) were allied with tsarism on the side of reaction. Engels did not try to grasp the social causes of the 'Vendean' role played by these national movements in 1848, but simply deduced it from their supposed 'counter-revolutionary' nature. The failure of the 1848 revolutions had precise causes, which were not at all the 'Vendean' nature of the Southern Slavs. Rather, this defeat was linked to a historical context: an epoch in which the European bourgeoisie had exhausted its revolutionary potential (being unable to solve the main problems on the agenda: the national and agrarian questions) and the proletariat was not yet ready to take power. In other words, it was too late for a bourgeois revolution and too soon for a socialist revolution.[25]

Engels's theory of peoples 'without history' was brilliantly criticised by Roman Rosdolsky, who proved its basic inconsistency. He explains the reactionary role played by the Slavonic national movements during the uprisings of 1848 in the light of the intrinsic contradictions of the revolution in Eastern Europe: some nations who fought for their own liberation, like Poland and Hungary, oppressed other nationalities and ethnic minorities in their own ranks. The leading social forces of the Polish and Magyar movements were the bourgeoisie and gentry, opposed to the other 'peasant nations'. The Ruthenians (Ukrainians) of Galicia, for example, did not support the demand for Polish independence, because they were already defending their own, embryonic national identity, a national identity which even expressed their *class conflict* with the Polish landowners. Serbs, Croats, Romanians, Slovaks and all the other 'peasant nations' of Southeastern Europe took the same attitude towards the Germans and Magyars. In reality, these so-called 'non-historical peoples' would have participated in the revolution if they had obtained a land reform from the bourgeoisie and gentry, but the chauvinist and conservative leadership of the German, Polish and Magyar national movements would not accept this and pushed the peasant masses into the arms of the tsarist counter-revolution.

Instead of grasping – with a Marxist method – the social roots of the Panslavic movement, Engels drew a map of Europe based on two categories: 'revolutionary nations' and 'peoples without history', the first viewed as historically viable, the second regarded as dead fragments of the past. This position, which denies *a priori* the possibility of a new awakening of the 'peoples without history', is completely antidialectical. Rosdolsky proves, with a long list of citations, that even after 1848 Engels retained his view of the revolution in East-Central Europe as a basically *German* revolution, with the same allies (in the first place the Poles) and the same enemies (tsarist Russia and the Panslavic movement).[26]

As early as the end of the nineteenth century, facing the birth of the socialist movement in the Balkan countries, Kautsky denounced Engels' mistake.[27] In 1907, in his great work on the national question, Otto Bauer criticised Engels, recognising the social and cultural development of the different Slavonic nationalities (that is, their adaptation to modern life).[28] In his critique, Rosdolsky introduces another argument: he explains that during Cromwell's revolution the Irish – whose national rights were justly supported by Marx and Engels – played no less reactionary a role than the Austrian Slavs in 1848. Nevertheless, they later built a national anti-imperialist movement. Through a critique of the *Neue Reinische Zeitung*'s attitude, Rosdolsky elaborates a brilliant Marxist analysis of the national question in the 1848 revolution. Far from falling again, as Nimni thinks, into Engels' 'paradigmatic trap' of the 'historical and non-historical nations', he comes to a very clear conclusion: the theory of the *geschichtlosen Völker* is nothing but 'a residue of the idealistic conception of history and therefore a foreign body in the theoretical system of Marxism'.[29] We can agree with Nimni's statement that the attitude of Engels towards the South Slavonic nations reveals some elements of positivistic evolutionism, economic determinism and Eurocentrism. Marx's friend doubtless internalised the cultural prejudices of nineteenth-century Europe, but it would be wrong to generalise this attitude: the concept of 'people without history' represents only *an aspect* of Engels' approach to the national question.

From the end of the nineteenth century on, Marxist ideas spread widely among the ethnic extra-territorial minorities and so-called 'non-historical nations' of East-Central Europe. The workers' movement and socialist intelligentsia of these nations found in Marxist theory the best intellectual instrument to explain their oppression, to grasp the historical process of formation of their cultural identity and, finally, to elaborate a project of both social and national liberation. The concept of cultural-national autonomy was created first of all by the Marxist currents of such oppressed nationalities as the Slavs (the Slavonic Federation of Austrian Social Democracy), the Jews (the Bund) and the Armenians (the 'Specifists'). The socialists of Ukraine (Rosdolsky), Bohemia (Smeral), Bulgaria (Blagoev), Romania (Dobrogeanu-Gherea), Georgia (Jordania), as well as Austrian-Slavonic (Etbin) and Russian-Jewish (Medem, Borokhov) socialists used Marxism to analyse their different national realities.[30] The theory of peoples 'without history' appeared to them as totally wrong and useless, but this was not a good reason for rejecting the Marxist theory of the national question as a whole. In the years between the world wars, the Spanish Marxists who were most instrumental in developing the theoretical analysis of the national question were Andreu Nin, a Catalan, and the Arenilla brothers, two Basques.[31] If the Marxist debate on the national question was carried forward, after Engels's death, above all by the socialists among ethnic minorities and oppressed nations, this means that the classical Marxist writings on this matter had some limitations and did not resolve the problem (that much is obvious), but also that Marxist theory was indispensable in order to confront national issues.

A Key Dichotomy

In conclusion, if the concept of nation elaborated by Marx and Engels is vague and incomplete, if Engels's theory of the 'non-historical' peoples is a pseudo-historicist metaphysics totally foreign to Marxism, what remains of their reflections on the national problem? We shall attempt now to synthesise the classical Marxist approach.

In 1867, when they returned to the Irish question, Marx and Engels acquired a basic theoretical point: *the dichotomy of dominant/oppressed nations.* They saw in the colonial domination of Ireland not only the source of the Irish people's oppression, but also the key for explaining the impotence of the English working class, the most numerous and organised proletariat of the world in the second half of the nineteenth century. The chauvinism and feelings of national superiority of the English workers towards the Irish were nourished by the British bourgeoisie, which exploited this antagonism in order to maintain its rule in Ireland and oppress the English proletariat. Marx wrote in 1870:

> Every industrial and commercial center in England now possesses a working class *divided* into two *hostile* camps, English proletarians and Irish proletarians. The ordinary English worker hates the Irish worker as a competitor who lowers his standard of life. In relation to the Irish worker he feels himself a member of the *ruling* nation and so turns himself into a tool of the aristocrats and capitalists *against Ireland,* thus strengthening their domination *over himself* ... This antagonism is *the secret of the impotence of the English working class,* despite its organisation. It is the secret by which the capitalist class maintains its power. And that class is fully aware of it.[32]

Marx thus formulated two concepts which would become the basis of Lenin's theory of national self-determination: 1. the nation that oppresses another cannot be free (Engels considered it a 'misfortune' for a people to rule over another); and 2. the liberation of the oppressed nation is a premiss for the socialist revolution in the dominant nation itself.

Today, this approach still retains its importance and validity and remains an absolutely necessary premiss for the development and theoretical enrichment of Marxism. This methodological approach is neither economic determinist nor Eurocentric, but simply represents an irreplaceable compass for those who believe in internationalism. We cannot consider ourselves Marxists if we do not support the right of self-determination of New Caledonia's Kanaks in France, of Palestinians in Israel, of Kosovo's Albanians in Yugoslavia, of Kurds in Iran, Iraq, Syria and Turkey; and last but not least, if we do not struggle in the US against US military intervention in other countries. If Ephraim Nimni agrees – as we hope he does – with this conclusion, he must recognise that it is possible to criticise Marx's and Engels's approaches to the national question without rejecting Marxism.

CHAPTER 3

The Marxist Debate on Self-Determination

The national question is one of the fields in which Lenin greatly developed Marxist theory, by spelling out (on the basis of Marx's writings, but going far beyond them) a coherent, revolutionary strategy for the workers' movement, based on the fundamental slogan of national self-determination. In its coherence and realism, the Leninist doctrine was far in advance of the positions of other Marxists of the period, even those closest to Lenin on this question: Kautsky and Stalin.

Kautsky's position prior to 1914 was similar to Lenin's, but was distinguished by its unilateral and almost exclusive concentration on language as the basis of the nation and by a lack of clarity and boldness in the formulation of the right of nations to secession. After 1914, the ambiguous and contradictory positions of Kautsky on the rights of nations in the context of the war were violently denounced by Lenin as 'hypocritical' and 'opportunist'.

The 'radical left' current (*Linksradikale*) represented by Rosa Luxemburg and Trotsky (before 1917) was characterised, to varying degrees and sometimes in very different forms, by its opposition to national separatism in the name of the principle of proletarian internationalism. Moreover, its stance on the national question was one of the principal differences between this current and Lenin, to whom it was close in its Marxist and revolutionary approach.

Luxemburg

In 1893 Rosa Luxemburg founded the Social Democratic Party of the Kingdom of Poland (SDKP), with a Marxist and internationalist programme, as a counter to the Polish Socialist Party (PPS), whose aim was to fight for the independence of Poland. Denouncing the PPS (with some justification) as a social-patriotic party, Luxemburg and her comrades of the SDKP were resolutely opposed to the slogan of independence for Poland and stressed, on the contrary, the close link between the Russian and Polish proletariats and their common destiny. The 'Kingdom of Poland' (part of Poland annexed to the tsarist empire), they said, should proceed towards territorial autonomy, not towards independence, within the framework of a future Russian democratic republic.

In 1896 Luxemburg represented the SDKP at the Congress of the Second International. The positions for which she argued in her intervention were set out in a subsequent article:[1] the liberation of Poland is as utopian as the liberation of Czechoslovakia, Ireland or Alsace-Lorraine. The unifying political struggle of the proletariat should not be supplanted by a 'series of fruitless national struggles'. The theoretical bases for this position were to be provided by the research she did for her doctoral thesis, *The Industrial Development of Poland*.[2] The central theme of this work was that, from the economic point of view, Poland was already integrated into Russia. The industrial growth of Poland was being achieved thanks to Russian markets and, consequently, the Polish economy could no longer exist in isolation from the Russian economy. Polish independence was the aspiration of the feudal Polish nobility; now industrial development had undermined the basis of this aspiration. Neither the Polish bourgeoisie, whose economic future depended on the Russian economy, nor the Polish proletariat, whose historic interests lay in a revolutionary alliance with the Russian proletariat, was nationalist. Only the petty bourgeoisie and the pre-capitalist layers still cherished the utopian dream of a united, independent Poland. In this respect, Luxemburg considered her book to be the Polish equivalent of Lenin's *The Development of Capitalism in Russia*,[3] which was directed against the utopian and retrogressive aspirations of the Russian populists.

Her most controversial statement on the national question (which Lenin, in particular, attacked) was the 1908–09 series of articles published under the title 'The National Question and Autonomy' in the journal of the Polish social-democratic party (which had become the SDKPiL, after a Lithuanian Marxist group had joined). The main – and most debatable – ideas put forward in these articles were the following: 1. the right of self-determination is an *abstract* and *metaphysical* right such as the so-called 'right to work' advocated by the nineteenth-century Utopians or the laughable 'right of every man to eat from gold plates' proclaimed by the writer Chernishevsky; 2. support for the right of secession of each nation implies in reality support for *bourgeois* nationalism: the nation as a uniform and homogenous entity does not exist – each class in the nation has conflicting interests and 'rights'; 3. the independence of small nations in general, and Poland in particular, is utopian from the economic point of view and condemned by the laws of history. For Luxemburg, there was only one exception to this rule: the Balkan nations of the Turkish empire (Greeks, Serbs, Bulgarians, Armenians). These nations had reached a degree of economic, social and cultural development superior to Turkey, a decadent empire whose dead weight oppressed them. From 1896 on (following a Greek national uprising on the island of Crete) Luxemburg considered – in contrast to the position defended by Marx at the time of the Crimean War – that the Turkish empire was not viable and that its decomposition into nation-states was necessary for historical progress.

To back up her views on the lack of future for small nations, Luxemburg used Engels's articles on 'non-historic nations' (though she attributed them to Marx: their true authorship was in fact only established in 1913, with the discovery of unpublished Marx–Engels letters). In particular, she used an article of January 1849 on the Hungarian struggle, quoting a passage about 'relics of a nation mercilessly trampled under foot in the course of history'.[4] She recognised that Engels's views on the Southern Slavs were mistaken, but she believed his method was correct and praised his 'sober realism, alien to all sentimentalism' as well as his contempt for the '"metaphysical" rights of nations'.[5]

As is well known, in 1914 Luxemburg was one of the few leaders of the Second International who did not succumb to the great wave of social patriotism which engulfed Europe with the advent of war. Imprisoned by the German authorities for her internationalist and anti-militarist propaganda, in 1915 she wrote and smuggled out of prison her famous *Junius Pamphlet*. In this text Luxemburg to some extent adopted the principle of self-determination: 'socialism gives to every people the right of independence and the freedom of independent control of its own destinies'.[6] However, for her this self-determination could not be exercised within existing capitalist states, particularly colonialist states. How could one speak of 'free choice' in relation to imperialist states like France, Turkey or tsarist Russia? In the age of imperialism the struggle for the 'national interest' is a mystification, not only in relation to the large colonial powers, but also for the small nations which are 'only the pawns on the imperialist chessboard of the great powers'.[7]

Luxemburg's theories on the national question, developed between 1893 and 1917, are based on four fundamental theoretical, methodological and political errors.

1. Particularly before 1914, she adopted an economist approach to the problem: Poland is economically dependent on Russia, therefore cannot be politically independent – an argument which tends to ignore the specificity and the relative individuality of each political situation. This determinist-economist method is particularly striking in her doctoral thesis and her early writings on the Polish question: the industrial development of Poland, linked to the Russian market, determines 'with the iron strength of historical necessity' (an expression which Luxemburg frequently used at this time, together with another of the same type: 'with the inevitability of natural law') on the one hand, the utopian nature of Polish independence and, on the other hand, the unity between the Russian and Polish proletariats. A characteristic example of this unmediated assimilation of politics to economics occurs in an article she wrote in 1902 on social patriotism, which stressed that the economic tendency – 'and therefore' the political tendency – in Poland was for union with Russia; the phrase 'and therefore' was an expression of this lack of mediation, which was not demonstrated but simply assumed to be self-evident.[8] However, this type of argument began to disappear as Luxemburg increasingly succeeded in avoiding the economist

trap, particularly after 1914, when she coined the phrase 'socialism or barbarism' (*Junius Pamphlet*) which represented a fundamental methodological break with fatalistic, Kautsky-type economism. Her arguments on the national question in the *Junius Pamphlet* were essentially political and not based on any mechanistic preconception.

2. For Luxemburg the nation was essentially a cultural phenomenon. Again, this tends to play down its political dimension, which cannot be equated simply with economy or ideology and whose concrete form is the independent nation-state (or the struggle to establish it). This is why Luxemburg was in favour of abolishing national oppression and allowing 'free cultural development', but refused to countenance separatism or the right to political independence. She did not understand that the denial of the right to form an independent nation-state is precisely one of the main forms of national oppression.

3. Luxemburg saw only the anachronistic, petty-bourgeois and reactionary aspects of national liberation movements and did not grasp their revolutionary potential against tsarism (and later, in another context, against imperialism and colonialism). In other words, she did not understand the complex and contradictory dialectic of the *dual nature* of these nationalist movements. With regard to Russia, in general she underestimated the revolutionary role of the non-proletarian allies of the working class: the peasantry, the oppressed nations. She saw the Russian Revolution as *purely* working-class and not – like Lenin – as *led* by the proletariat.[9]

4. She failed to understand that the national liberation of oppressed nations is not only a demand of the 'utopian', 'reactionary' and 'pre-capitalist' petty bourgeoisie, but also of *the masses as a whole,* including the proletariat; and that, therefore, the recognition by the Russian proletariat of the right of nations to self-determination was an *indispensable condition* of its solidarity with the proletariat of oppressed nations.

What was the source of these mistakes, inconsistencies and shortcomings? It would be wrong to think that they were logically linked to Luxemburg's method (apart from pre-1914 economism) or to her political positions as a whole (for example, on the party, democracy, etc.). In fact, these theories on the national question were not peculiar to Luxemburg, but were shared by the other leaders of the SDKPiL, even those who, like Dzerzhinsky, supported Bolshevism. It is most likely that Luxemburg's one-sided position was, in the last analysis, an ideological by-product of the continual, intense and bitter ideological struggle of the SDKPiL against the PPS.[10]

The difference between Lenin and Luxemburg was, therefore, to a certain extent (at least as regards Poland) a result of the different standpoints of the Russian internationalists (struggling to defeat Great Russian chauvinism) and the Polish internationalists (combating Polish social patriotism). Lenin at one time seemed to recognise a certain 'division of labour' between Russian and Polish Marxists on this question. Having said this, his major criticism of Luxemburg was that she tried to generalise from a certain specific situation (Poland at a particular point in history) and therefore to deny not just Polish independence, but that of all other small oppressed nations.

However, in one article Luxemburg stated the problem in terms very similar to Lenin's: the 1905 Introduction to the collection *The Polish Question and the Socialist Movement*. In this essay, Luxemburg made a careful distinction between the undeniable *right* of every nation to independence ('which flowed directly from the most elementary principles of socialism'), which she recognised, and the *desirability* of this independence for Poland, which she denied. This is also one of the few texts in which she recognised the importance, depth and even justification of national feelings (though treating them as merely a 'cultural' phenomenon) and stressed that national oppression is the 'most intolerably barbaric oppression' and can only arouse 'wrathful, fanatical rebellion'.[11] This work, together with certain passages in the *Junius Pamphlet*, shows that Luxemburg's thought was too realistic, in the revolutionary sense of the word, simply to present a linear coherence of a metaphysical and rigid kind.

Trotsky

Trotsky's writings on the national question prior to 1917 can be defined as 'eclectic' (the word Lenin used to criticise them), occupying a half-way position between Luxemburg and Lenin. It was in particular after 1914 that Trotsky became interested in the national question. He took it up in his pamphlet *The War and the International* (1914) – a polemical work directed against social patriotism – from two different – if not contradictory – standpoints.

A historical-economic approach

The world war was a product of the contradiction between the productive forces, which tend towards a world economy, and the restrictive framework of the nation-state. Trotsky therefore heralded 'the destruction of the nation state *as an independent economic entity*' – which, from the strictly economic point of view, was a totally justifiable proposition. However, he deduced from this premiss the 'collapse' (*Zusammenbruch*) and the 'destruction' (*Zertrummerung*) of the nation-state *altogether*; the nation-state as such, the very concept of the nation, would only be able to exist in the future as a 'cultural, ideological and psychological phenomenon'. Of course, this was an evident *non sequitur*. The ending of the economic independence of a nation-state is in no way synonymous with the disappearance of the nation-state as a political entity. Like Luxemburg, Trotsky tended to reduce the nation either to economics or to culture and thus lost sight of the specifically political aspect of the problem: the nation-state as a political phenomenon, distinct from the economic or ideological spheres (though, of course, having mediated relations with both).

A concrete political approach

Unlike Luxemburg, Trotsky explicitly proclaimed the right of nations to self-determination as one of the conditions for 'peace between nations', which he contrasted with 'the peace of the diplomats'. Moreover, he supported the perspective of an independent and united Poland (free from tsarist, Austrian and German domination) as well as the independence of Hungary, Romania, Bulgaria, Serbia, Bohemia, etc. It was in the liberation of these nations and their association in a Balkan federation that he saw the best barrier to tsarism in Europe. Furthermore, with remarkable perception Trotsky demonstrated the dialectical relationship between proletarian internationalism and national rights: the destruction of the International by the social patriots was a crime not just against socialism, but against the 'national interest, in its widest and correct sense', since it dissolved the only force capable of reconstructing Europe on the basis of democratic principles and the right of nations to self-determination.[12]

In a series of articles in 1915 ('Nation and Economy'),[13] Trotsky tried to define the national question in a more precise way, but not without a certain ambiguity. The contradictory lines of his argument were indicative of a thought which had not yet crystallised. He began with a polemic against the social imperialists, who justified their political position by the need to expand markets and productive forces. This polemic, from the methodological point of view, seemed to reject economism: yes, Marxists are in favour of the greatest possible expansion in the economic sphere, but not at the expense of dividing, disorganising and weakening the workers' movement. Trotsky's argument was somewhat confused, in that he wrote of the workers' movement as 'the most important productive force in modern society'; nevertheless, what he did was to affirm the overriding importance of a *political* criterion. However, throughout both articles he returned to the 'centralising needs of economic development', which call for the destruction of the nation-state as a hindrance to the expansion of productive forces. How could these 'needs' be reconciled with the right of nations to self-determination, which Trotsky also recognised? He escaped this dilemma by means of a theoretical somersault which led him back into economism: '[T]he state is essentially an economic organisation, it will be forced to adapt to the needs of economic development.' Therefore, the nation-state would be dissolved into the 'Republican United States of Europe', while the nation, divorced from the economy and freed from the old framework of the state, would have the right to self-determination ... in the sphere of 'cultural development'.

In 1917 Trotsky abandoned these 'eclectic' positions and adopted the Leninist conception of the national question, which he brilliantly defended at Brest-Litovsk in his capacity as People's Commissar for Foreign Affairs.

Stalin

Stalin's pre-1917 positions on the national question cannot be entirely identified with Lenin's either. It is true that it was Lenin who sent Stalin to Vienna to write his famous article 'Marxism and the National Question',[14] and that in a letter to Maxim Gorky in February 1913 he spoke of the 'marvellous Georgian who has sat down to write a big article'.[15] But once the article was finished, it does not appear (contrary to a popular myth) that Lenin was particularly enthusiastic about it, as he does not mention it in any of his numerous writings on the national question, apart from a brief, parenthetical reference in passing in an article dated 28 December 1913. It is obvious that the main ideas in Stalin's work were those of the Bolshevik Party and Lenin. Having said this, Trotsky's suggestion that the article was inspired, supervised and corrected 'line by line' by Lenin seems questionable.[16] On the contrary, on a certain number of fairly important points Stalin's work implicitly and explicitly differs from, and even contradicts, Lenin's writings.

1. The concept of 'national character', of 'common psychological make-up' or 'psychological particularity' of nations *is not at all Leninist*. This problematic is a legacy from Bauer, whom Lenin explicitly criticised for his 'psychological theory'.[17] In fact, the idea of a national psychology has more in common with a certain superficial and pre-scientific folklore than with a Marxist analysis of the national question.

2. By baldly stating that 'it is only when all these characteristics (common language, territory, economic life and 'psychic formation') are present together that we have a nation', Stalin gave his theory a dogmatic, restrictive and rigid character which one never finds in Lenin. The Stalinist conception of a nation was a real ideological Procrustean bed. According to Stalin, Georgia before the second half of the nineteenth

century was not a nation, because it had no 'common
economic life', being divided into economically independent
principalities. There is no need to add that on this criterion
Germany, prior to the Customs Union, would not have been
a nation either ... . Nowhere in Lenin's writings do we find
such an ultimatist, rigid and arbitrary 'definition' of a nation.

3. Stalin explicitly refused to allow the possibility of the
unity or association of national groups scattered within a
multi-national state: 'The question arises: is it possible to
unite into a single national union groups that have grown so
distinct? ... Is it conceivable, that, for instance, the Germans of
the Baltic Provinces and the Germans of Trans-caucasia can
be "united into a single nation"?' The answer given, of course,
was that all this was 'not conceivable', 'not possible' and
'utopian'.[18] Lenin, by contrast, vigorously defended the
freedom of association, including the association of any
communities no matter what their nationality, in any given
State', citing as an example precisely the Germans of the
Caucasus, the Baltic and the Petrograd area. He added that
freedom of association of every kind between members of the
nation, scattered in different parts of the country or even the
globe, was 'indisputable, and can be argued against only from
the hidebound, bureaucratic point of view'.[19]

4. Stalin made no distinction between Great Russian tsarist
oppressive nationalism and the nationalism of oppressed
nations. In a very revealing paragraph in his article, he rejected
in one breath the 'warlike and repressive' nationalism of the
tsars 'from above' and the 'wave of nationalism from below
which sometimes turns into crass chauvinism' of the Poles,
Jews, Tatars, Georgians, Ukrainians, etc. Not only did he fail
to make any distinction between nationalism 'from above' and
'from below', but he aimed his most severe criticisms at social
democrats in oppressed countries who had not 'stood firm' in
the face of the nationalist movement. Lenin, on the other
hand, not only considered the difference between the nationalism of the oppressor and the oppressed nation to be
absolutely decisive, but always attacked most bitterly those
who capitulated, consciously or unconsciously, to Great
Russian national chauvinism. It is no accident that one of the
main targets of his polemic were the Marxist social democrats

of an oppressed nation, Poland, who by their 'firm' stand
against Polish nationalism ended up by denying Poland's right
to secede from the Russian empire. This difference between
Lenin and Stalin was highly significant and already contained
the germ of the later violent conflict between them on the
national question in Georgia (December 1922) – Lenin's
famous 'last fight'.

Lenin

Lenin's starting-point in working out a strategy on the national
question was the same as for Luxemburg and Trotsky: proletarian internationalism. However, Lenin understood better
than his comrades of the revolutionary left the dialectical relationship between internationalism and the right of national
self-determination. He understood, first, that only the *freedom*
to secede makes possible *free* and voluntary union, association,
cooperation and, in the long term, fusion between nations;
second, that only the recognition by the workers' movement in
the oppressor nation of the right of the oppressed nation to
self-determination can help to eliminate the hostility and
suspicion of the oppressed and unite the proletariat of both
nations in the international struggle against the bourgeoisie.

Similarly, Lenin grasped the dialectical relationship
between national-democratic struggles and the socialist revolution and showed that the popular masses (not just the proletariat but also the peasantry and petty bourgeoisie) of the
oppressed nation were the allies of the conscious proletariat: a
proletariat whose task it would be to lead the struggle of this
'disparate, discordant and heterogenous mass', containing
elements of the petty bourgeoisie and backward workers with
their 'preconceptions, reactionary fantasies, weaknesses and
errors', against capitalism and the bourgeois state.[20] It is true,
however, that in relation to Russia it was only really after April
1917, when Lenin adopted the strategy of permanent revolution, that he began to see the national liberation struggle of
oppressed nations within the Russian empire not only as a
democratic movement, but as an ally of the proletariat in the
Soviet *socialist* revolution.

From the methodological point of view, Lenin's principal superiority over most of his contemporaries was his capacity to 'put politics in command', his obstinate, inflexible, constant and unflinching tendency to grasp and highlight the *political* aspect of every problem and every contradiction. This tendency stood out in his polemic against the Economists on the question of the Party in 1902–03; in his discussion with the Mensheviks on the question of the democratic revolution in 1905; in the originality of his writings on imperialism in 1916; in the inspired turn which the April Theses represented in 1917; in the whole of his most important work *State and Revolution* and, of course, in his writings on the national question. It is this methodological aspect which explains (among other things) the striking *actuality* of Lenin's ideas in the twentieth century, an age of imperialism, which has seen the political level become increasingly *dominant* (even though, in the last analysis, it is of course *determined* by the economic).

On the national question, while most other Marxist writers saw only the economic, cultural or 'psychological' dimension of the problem, Lenin stated clearly that the question of self-determination 'belongs wholly and exclusively to the sphere of political democracy',[21] that is, to the realm of the right of *political* secession and the establishment of an independent nation-state. What is more, Lenin was perfectly conscious of the methodological foundation of the differences: 'An "autonomous" nation does not enjoy rights equal to those of a "sovereign" nation; our Polish comrades could not have failed to notice this had they not (like our old Economists) obstinately avoided making an analysis of *political* concepts and categories.'[22] Thanks to Lenin's understanding of the relative autonomy of the political process, he was able to avoid both subjectivism and economism in his analysis of the national question.[23]

Needless to say, the political aspect of the national question for Lenin was not at all that with which chancelleries, diplomats and armies concern themselves. He was totally indifferent to whether this or that nation had an independent state or what the frontiers were between two states. His aim was *democracy* and the *internationalist unity* of the proletariat, which both require the recognition of the right of nations to self-determination.

What is more, precisely because it concentrates on the political aspect, his theory of self-determination makes absolutely no concession to nationalism. It is situated solely in the sphere of the democratic struggle and the proletarian revolution.

It is true that these two aims did not have equal importance in Lenin's eyes. Democratic demands always had to be subordinated to the overriding interests of the revolutionary class struggle of the world proletariat. For example, according to Lenin, if the republican movement turns out, in a particular case, to be an instrument of reaction (Cambodia 1971!), Marxists will not support it. This does not mean that the working-class movement must strike out republicanism from its programme. The same goes, *mutatis mutandis,* for self-determination. Even though there are some exceptions, the general rule is the right of secession for each nation. In fact, Lenin's analysis that the recognition of the right to self-determination is of primary importance in creating the conditions for internationalist unity among workers tends implicitly to exclude even the possibility of 'exceptions', of any contradiction between the interests of the proletariat and the democratic rights of nations.

Conclusion: The Lesson of History

Some of the specific debates among Marxists on aspects of the national question have been settled by history. The multinational state of Austria-Hungary broke up into several nation-states after the First World War. The Basques, 'an essentially reactionary nation' according to Engels, experienced with the fall of the Franco regime the most far-reaching radicalisation of any people in Spain. The reunification of Poland, which Luxemburg referred to as petty-bourgeois utopianism, became a reality in 1918. The 'non-historic' Czech nation, which was destined to disappear because of its lack of 'national vitality' (according to Engels), was the dominant nation in post-1918 Czechoslovakia and has its own separate state today.

The experience of post-1917 history also shows us that the nation is not simply a collection of abstract, external criteria.

The subjective element, the consciousness of a national identity and a national political movement, is no less important. Obviously these 'subjective factors' do not come out of the blue; they are the result of certain historical conditions – persecution, oppression, etc. But this means that self-determination must have a wider application; it must relate not just to secession, but to the 'national entity' itself. It is not a doctrinaire 'expert' armed with a list of 'objective criteria' (of the Stalin type) who will determine whether a community constitutes a nation or not, but *the community itself.*[24]

On the other hand, ever since Woodrow Wilson, the nationalism of the great powers has re-stocked its ideological arsenal by appropriating the slogans of democracy, equality of nations and the right of self-determination. These principles are now proclaimed by bourgeois statesmen everywhere. Lyndon Johnson, when president of the US, declared solemnly in 1966: 'We are fighting to uphold the principle of self-determination, so that the people of South Vietnam may be free to choose their own future.'[25] Since the nineteenth century – when Treitschke wrote, on the occasion of an uprising in Africa: 'It is pure mockery to apply normal principles of war in wars with savages. A negro tribe must be chastised by setting its villages on fire, because this is the only kind of remedy that is effective'[26] – how the policy of the great powers in relation to small nations has changed out of all recognition!

The real threat today to the political health of the workers' movement is not the infantile disorder which Luxemburg's generous errors represented. Indeed, 'ultra-leftism' on the national question hardly survives today. Only in certain sectors of the revolutionary Left does one still sometimes find a distant echo of Luxemburg's theses, in the form of an abstract opposition to national liberation movements in the name of 'working-class unity' and internationalism. The same is true with respect to Engels's notion of 'reactionary nations'.

Thus, if one looks at certain of the national questions of today, complex questions where national, colonial, religious and ethnic aspects combine and interlace – for example, the Arab–Israeli conflict or the struggle between Catholics and Protestants in Northern Ireland – one can see that there are two contrary temptations which haunt the revolutionary Left. The first temptation is to deny the legitimacy of the national movement of Palestinians or of Catholics in Ulster: to condemn these movements as 'petty-bourgeois' and divisive of the working class and to proclaim abstractly against them the principle of the necessary unity between proletarians of all nationalities, races or religions. The second temptation is to espouse uncritically the nationalist ideology of these movements and condemn the dominant nations (Israeli Jews or Northern Irish Protestants) en bloc, without distinction of class, as 'reactionary nations' – nations to which the right of self-determination is denied.

The task facing revolutionary Marxists is to avoid these twin reefs and discover – through a concrete analysis of each concrete situation – an authentically internationalist course, which draws its inspiration from the nationalities policy of the Comintern when it was led by Lenin and Trotsky (1919–23) and from the famous resolution of the Second International's 1896 Congress whose rare privilege it was to be approved by both Lenin and Luxemburg:

> The Congress proclaims the full right to self-determination of all nations; and it expresses its sympathy to the workers of all countries at present suffering beneath the yoke of military, national or any other kind of absolutism; the Congress calls on the workers of these countries to join the ranks of the conscious workers of the whole world, in order to struggle beside them to defeat international capitalism and attain the goals of international social democracy.

CHAPTER 4

The Nation as a Common Fate: Otto Bauer Today[1]

Even if Marxists have often underestimated the importance of national problems, there are nonetheless contributions of great value, even indispensable ones, to be found in this field in Marxist writings. This is the case notably with Otto Bauer's 'classic' work, *The Question of Nationalities and Social Democracy*.

First published in 1907, this book arose in a specific historical and political context: the attempt by the Austro-Marxist current – represented by the Austrian Social-Democratic Party – to save the multi-national framework of the Austro-Hungarian state by means of a reform that would grant all its nationalities (Hungarians, Germans, Czechs, Slovaks, Croats, etc.) 'national-cultural autonomy': it would have given each national community the chance to organize itself as a legal public corporation, granted a certain degree of cultural, administrative and legal authority.[2]

As we know, this programme was doomed to fail. Following the empire's military defeat and the 1918 revolution, the Austro-Hungarian multi-national state fell apart into several independent states. As early as January 1918, Bauer observed the inadequacy of this strategy in the face of the rise of national aspirations. He proposed, in the programme of the Left that he was drafting at the time, to recognise peoples' rights to self-determination (and therefore to creating separate states).

That said, we can legitimately pose the question today, given the mushrooming of separatist or expansionist movements eager for 'national homogeneity', whether regional autonomy and cultural autonomy (in the framework of multi-national federations based on voluntary membership) are not often a more rational and more humane solution. While the democratic right to self-determination is indispensable, how can it be applied to territories where nations are thoroughly intermixed without setting off battles, massacres and 'ethnic cleansing'?

Be that as it may, the importance of Bauer's book goes beyond the framework of the concrete political strategy that he proposed to deal with the complex national questions in Central Europe. It consists above all in the original concepts and lucid analyses that he developed in order to make the national phenomenon intelligible and do justice to its socio-historical nature.

None of this contradicts the fact that his analyses include weaknesses and limits that were typical of his epoch and cultural milieu. As Claudie Weill reminds us in her preface to the French translation of his book, Bauer shared a whole mental universe with other Marxists of the Second International. In order to oppose metaphysical theories of the nation, he found it useful to appeal to Darwin and the principles of natural selection. Similarly, his vision of the future of nations was not free from 'illusions of progress'.[3] This was particularly evident in his remarks on the Jewish nation, whose rapid assimilation he predicted – as did so many other Marxists (notably Jews!) – though this did not stop the Jewish socialists of the Bund from appropriating his analyses and his programme of national-cultural autonomy.[4] Generally speaking he did not foresee at all the dangers that the rise of nationalism could lead to. But who at the dawn of the twentieth century could imagine the world wars and genocides in the name of 'the nation' (and/or 'the race'), one after another without let-up, that would make this century one of the most gruesome in human history?

Despite these failings – and the rather problematic nature of the concept of 'national character', which had a privileged place in his theoretical arsenal – Bauer's work remains a monument of critical intelligence and humanist rationalism. By defining the nation as a 'common historical fate', as the 'never completed product of an unending process',[5] he occupies a position of irreconcilable opposition to national conservatism, reactionary myths of the 'eternal nation', and racist ideology.

Denouncing 'fetishisation of national character' – doctrines
that exalted the national reality into an unchanging, constant
essence – Bauer treated nations as *open historical realities*:

> There is no moment when a nation's history is complete. As
> events transform this character, which is obviously nothing
> more than a condensation of past destiny, they subject it to
> continual changes ... . Through this process national char-
> acter also loses its supposed *substantial character*, that is, the
> illusion that national character is the fixed element in the
> confusion of events ... . Placed in the middle of the
> universal flux, it is no longer a persistent *being*, but a
> continual process of *becoming* and disappearing.[6]

Thanks to this eminently *dialectical* method, Bauer decon-
structs *metaphysical* concepts of the nation: both what he calls
'national materialism', which claims that a hereditary and
unchanging racial substance is the basis of a nation (Gobineau),
and 'national spiritualism', which attributes the behaviour of
individuals belonging to the same nation to some mysterious
'genius of the people' – explaining for example 'Kohn's,
Meyer's, Löwy's and other people's tendency to abstraction' as
a manifestation of 'the spirit of the Jewish people'.[7]

This *historicist* stance (in the sense that Lukács or Gramsci
would use the term) gives Bauer's book a real methodological
superiority, not only relative to other Austro-Marxist writers
like Karl Renner (whose approach was too legalistic and
administrative) but also relative to other Marxists of his time,
whose writings on the national question are too economistic or
too abstract and rigid – like the four-point definition in Stalin's
famous pamphlet, which would become a real Procrustean
bed and a serious obstacle to concrete thinking.

In so far as Bauer's method implies both a historical explanation of existing national configurations and an understanding of nations as processes, as movements of permanent
transformation, it also makes it possible to overcome the
mistake Engels made in 1848–50. The fact that a nation (like
the Czechs) 'had no history' (as an independent state) does
not necessarily mean that it has no future. The development
of capitalism led in Central Europe and the Balkans not to the

assimilation but to the reawakening of supposedly 'non-historic' nations. (Curiously, Bauer did not extend this analysis to the Jewish case.)

What is a nation? Bauer has no hesitation in Chapter 10 of his book in proposing a 'complete definition': 'A nation is a set of human beings linked by a common fate and common character.'[8] Let us try to examine this concept of a 'common fate' (*Schicksalsgemeinschaft*) more closely, since it plays a central role in his theory. Georges Haupt rightly observes that Bauer's methodological premisses lead him to combine Neo-Kantian categories with historical materialist ones: 'He borrows from Neo-Kantianism the principle of national individuality, which includes the historically forged specificity and historic permanence of a nation. He resorts to Marxism in order to define, in terms of class, relations and forces of production, the content, nature, and social forces involved in changes that occur.'[9]

But even more important than Neo-Kantianism for Bauer's theoretical tool kit is the contribution of German sociology, and in particular Ferdinand Tönnies, whose famous work *Gemeinschaft und Gesellschaft* (*Community and Society*, 1887) is doubtless the immediate source of Bauer's concept of a *community* of fate. For Tönnies a community is founded on an 'essential will' (*Wesenswille*), while a society is structured by an 'arbitrary will' (*Kürwille*). While a *Gemeinschaft* (family, clan, village) is governed by customs, mores and rites, by relations of mutual aid and mutual trust, and unified by a common *Kultur* (religion, art, morality), a *Gesellschaft* (city, factory, country) is driven by calculation, gain, profit, contract and competition in the context of the irreversible development of *Zivilisation* (technical, scientific and industrial progress).

Bauer acknowledges his debt to Tönnies' 'excellent work' in a footnote, but gives a somewhat different meaning to the two concepts of German sociology.

> I see the foundation of a *Gesellschaft* in human cooperation under outside governance; and the foundation of a *Gemeinschaft* in what individuals are ... the result of countless interactions between themselves and other individuals joined in a community, and thus, in their individual characters, a manifestation of the collective character.[10]

Bauer's 'common fate' thus shares with Tönnies' community the idea of historic organism and of an internal cultural unity rooted in common experience.

Attempts to define nations on the basis of language alone (for example in Karl Kautsky's work) are based in Bauer's eyes on a superficial view of national realities, which dissolves *community* into *society*. 'The opinion that national diversities are nothing more than linguistic diversities depends on an *individualistic-atomistic conception of society,* in which a society appears to be no more than a set of individuals joined together in an external way, for example by language.'[11]

Similarly, Bauer rejects any fetishising of *territory*: in so far as there is a common culture, despite geographical distance, individuals can belong to the same nation: for example in the case of immigrants who remain in their new country attached to their original culture. Only in cases where a common soil is a pre-condition for a common culture is it a pre-condition for the existence of a nation.[12]

Because of his rejection of fixed criteria and rigid definitions, Bauer is, in the field of the Marxist theory of the nation, *the anti-Stalin par excellence.* His concept of the nation as a common fate allows us to take account of the national identity of communities that, because of their lack of a common territory or distinct language, do not fit into abstract definitions and classifications: for example Jews or African-Americans. A collective memory of persecution, exclusion or massacres creates a national community of fate and thus contributes in a decisive way to forging this identity.

What may be missing in Bauer's concept of the nation is a clear picture of the role of *imagination* in forming a community of fate. If nations are to a large extent *imagined communities* (Benedict Anderson) or *cultural creations* (Eric Hobsbawm),[13] then the subjective dimension of national identity, the imaginary reconstruction of the past, the ever-new reinterpretation of history, are constituent elements of a community of fate just as much as 'objective' historical events are.

A subtle and pluralist analyst of nationalities, Bauer is nonetheless hostile to nationalism, which he refers to with the term 'national valorisation' ('that is, the fact that we consider something good because it is German, whatever it is'). He considers nationalism a tool of the ruling and possessing classes in legitimating existing institutions. He counterposes to this ideology what he calls *rationalist evaluation,* which is made in relation to a higher goal or ideal, represented in German culture by thinkers who rejected nationalism: Herder, Lessing, Heine. In his eyes the workers' movement was both charged with a major national task (appropriation by the people of a national culture reserved until now for the elite) and inspired by 'rationalist evaluation' in all its theory and practice. He also praised 'cultural cross-breeding', for example in Karl Marx's thought, which was the result of a condensation of four nations' histories: Jewish, German, English and French.[14]

In short, despite his belief in the need for national differentiation among socialist movements and his proposal to root socialist culture in the specific culture of each country, he remained in the last analysis an *internationalist.* 'International socialism', he wrote in the 1924 preface to a new edition of his book, 'must perceive this national differentiation in the methods of struggle and ideology in its ranks as the result of external and internal growth'. And he concluded with this appeal: 'The International's duty can and must be, not to level national particularities, but to promote international unity in national diversity.'[15]

In an epoch of the rise of nationalism, racism, xenophobia and 'ethnic cleansing', it is useful to be able to turn back to a thinker who recognised the crucial role and importance of nations and national cultures, but rejected their mystified distortions. The relevance of Bauer today results from his profoundly humanist spirit, which made him a worthy heir of the rationalism of Herder, Lessing, Heine and Marx.

CHAPTER 5

Nationalism and Internationalism

Over 200 years after the call for a universal brotherhood of all humankind issued by the great French Revolution and 80 years after the foundation of the Communist International, what remains of the great dream of internationalist solidarity of the oppressed? Hasn't nationalism always been the main moving force of world politics? And how should socialists relate to it?

The contradictory role of nationalism is one of the great paradoxes in the history of the twentieth century. At the service of the state and of reactionary forces, the ideology of nationalism fostered and legitimised some of the worst crimes of the century: two world wars, the genocide of Armenians, Jews and Gypsies, colonialist wars, the rise of fascism and military dictatorship, the brutal repression of progressive or revolutionary movements from China in the 1920s to Indonesia in the 1960s and Argentina in the 1970s.

On the other hand, in the name of national liberation, colonised peoples gained their independence and some of the most important and radical revolutionary socialist movements were able to win popular support and triumph: in Yugoslavia, China, Indochina, Cuba and Nicaragua.

Another puzzling paradox: although nationalism has been the dominant factor in shaping twentieth-century politics, the greatest revolution of our times, October 1917, owed nothing to nationalism and was explicitly directed against the 'national defence of the fatherland' in the war with imperial Germany. Moreover, there has never been in the history of the labour and socialist movement a mass world organisation so thoroughly committed to internationalism as in the twentieth century: the Third International (at least during its first years of existence).

How should we understand these paradoxes? Can Marxism furnish the theoretical tools for such an understanding? Do the workers and the exploited really have no fatherland, as Marx thought in 1848? How far can Mother Earth become the concrete horizon for social liberation? And what are the perspectives for nationalism and internationalism in the twenty-first century?

Any attempt to answer these questions has to start with a dialectical approach to the problem: the national question is *contradictory,* and its contradictions are not the expression of some eternal trait of human nature, but of concrete *historical conditions.*

It is important to distinguish very carefully between the feeling of national identity, the attachment to a national culture, the consciousness of belonging to a national community with its own historical past – and *nationalism.* Nationalism as an ideology is composed of all these elements but also of something else, which is its decisive ingredient: the choice of the nation as *the* primary, fundamental and most important social and political value, to which all others are – in one way or another – subordinated. Hans Kohn, the well-known historian of modern nationalism, defined it as 'a state of mind, in which the supreme loyalty of the individual is felt to be due to the nation-state'.[1] This is a quite adequate definition – if one includes in it also the struggle *for the establishment* of the nation-state – even if one has to admit that there exist at least some (moderate) nationalist movements who aim only at cultural or territorial autonomy.

It is not easy to find out exactly how and when nationalism was born. Some authors see it as contemporary with the emergence of the modern nation-state in the fifteenth and sixteenth centuries (Machiavelli!). Others, like Kohn, relate it to the first great bourgeois revolutions: in England in the seventeenth century and France in 1789 for the first time the state 'ceased to be the king's state: it became the people's state, a national state, a fatherland'.[2] More recently Tom Nairn tried to prove that nationalism emerged in the nineteenth century (as a result of the uneven development of capitalism) in the peripheral countries (Germany, Italy and Japan) and only later reached the 'core areas' (England and France);[3] but this strange chronology is too arbitrary and seems to ignore such well-known historical facts as the patriotic dimension of the French

Revolution and of the Napoleonic wars. In any case there is no doubt that for many centuries the political ideal was not the nation or the nation-state, but other forms of social and political organisation: the clan, the city-state, the feudal lord, the church, the dynastic kingdom and the multi-national empire. And although some precedents can be found in the past (the ancient Hebrews or the ancient Greeks), they are of a quite different nature and substance from modern nationalism.

Marxist socialism is fundamentally opposed to nationalism. First of all because it refuses to see the nation as an undifferentiated bloc: all nations are divided into *different social classes,* with different interests and different conceptions of national identity. But above all it rejects the nationalist ideology and its scale of values because its supreme loyalty is not to any nation, but to an international historical subject (the proletariat) and to an international historical aim: the socialist transformation of the world. It is internationalist both for ethical and for material reasons.

The ethical motives are important: for the Marxist worldview, materialist and atheistic, the only value which can be considered 'sacred' – absolute – is humanity itself (of which the exploited and the oppressed are the emancipatory force). In this sense, the motto 'Workers of the world, unite!' is not only a practical proposal for action, but also the socialist ethical response to the 'sacred love of country' of nationalist ideology. Socialism is therefore an internationalist movement by virtue of the universalist and humanist character of its values and aims. Without this ethical appeal it is impossible to understand the total commitment and sacrifice of many generations of activists from the labour movements of many countries to international socialism (or communism). As the Old Bolshevik Adolf Yoffe wrote in his last letter to Trotsky in 1927 (before committing suicide): 'Human life has no meaning unless it is at the service of an infinite, which for us is humanity'.

However, if internationalism were only a moral principle, a categorical imperative, it would be easy to dismiss it as a beautiful utopia. If this is not the case, it is because proletarian internationalism draws its political force from objective, concrete and material conditions, already analysed by Marx in the *Manifesto*: the economic unification of the world by the capitalist system.

Like any dialectical totality, world capitalism is not the sum total of its parts, the national economies; nor is the international class struggle the sum total of national struggles. They constitute an organic whole, with its own forms of motion, distinct from the peculiarities of its component elements. Georg Lukács insisted in *History and Class Consciousness* that the category of totality was, on the methodological level, the carrier of the revolutionary principle. From the dialectical standpoint of totality, no local or national situation can be grasped in theory or transformed in practice if one ignores its links with the whole: with the world economic, social and political movement.

As a matter of fact, far from being anachronistic, Marx's analysis in the *Manifesto* is much more adequate *in our times* than in 1848. Imperialism has imposed on the world capitalist system a much higher degree of integration, the control of the market by multinational monopolies is incomparably greater; in short, the unification of the planet by the capitalist mode of production has achieved today a qualitatively higher level than in 1848. And this economic unity also has a political and military expression in Western Atlanticism, US interventionism, etc. This means that internationalism has its roots in the structure of the world economy and world politics. Socialist internationalism is *also* the consciousness of this objective reality.

What is the decisive factor in class struggle: national or international conditions? Should one privilege the importance of the world process or, as Mao once wrote, the internal factors and the national (endogenous) causes? In this problematic, the question itself is misleading. It supposes an abstract, metaphysical and static separation between the national and the international, the 'internal' and the 'external', the 'inside' and the 'outside'. The dialectical standpoint is precisely based on the understanding of the *contradictory unity* between the national economy and world market, national and international class struggle – unity which is visible already in the fact that (economic and social) national specificity is the product of the unequal development of international capitalism.

What *is* wrong in the *Manifesto* and others of Marx's writings is the idea that modern industrial capitalism is essentially a *homogenising* force, creating *identical* conditions of life and struggle among the exploited of all countries. His statement in 1845 that 'the nationality of the worker is neither French, nor English, nor German, it is *labour, free slavery, self-huckstering*'[4] has a large share of truth; but it ignores not only the cultural specificities of each nation (which capitalism does not abolish at all) but also socioeconomic differences between proletarians of different nations, which result from the *uneven and combined development of the world capitalist system.* Moreover, one cannot neglect the importance of national peculiarities for the 'making of the working class' in each country and for the development of its own tradition of anti-capitalist resistance and struggle.

In other words, although capitalism creates both in the industrial metropolis and in the dominated countries a modern proletariat which fights against the same enemy and has the same objective historical interests, this does not mean at all that its material and social conditions of life (not to mention its national cultures) are identical. As Leon Trotsky once wrote: 'If we take Britain and India as polarised varieties of the capitalist type, then we are obliged to say that the internationalism of the British and Indian proletariats does not at all rest on an *identity* of conditions, tasks and methods, but on their indivisible *interdependence.*'[5] World capitalism creates incredible inequalities and brutal differences in life conditions between the centre and periphery of the system: only the complementarity, the reciprocal relation of the struggles in the different countries can generate internationalist solidarity. Thus the anti-war movements in France in the 1950s and in the US in the 1960s and 1970s were a powerful contribution to the struggle of the Algerians and of the Indochinese people – and vice versa: these colonial struggles helped to ignite radical contestation in the metropolitan centres.

To sum up, internationalism is not the expression of the identity in life conditions of the exploited and oppressed of all countries, but of a dialectical relationship of complementarity between at least three very different kinds of struggles: the socialist labour movement in advanced capitalist

societies; social and national liberation movements in dependent (or colonial) capitalist countries; and movements for
democracy and against market 'reforms' in the former East
Bloc countries.

The Many Roots of Nationalism

Marxists have often underestimated the importance of the
national question, the decisive significance of national liberation for the dominated peoples. This is part of a general
pattern of blindness, neglect or at least insufficient attention to
non-class forms of oppression: national, racial or sexual. It is
not that Marxism as such is unable to take into account these
dimensions, but the economistic approach which dominated
much of Marxist thinking (and also some of Marx's own writings) led to a tendency to disregard them.

Marxists have also very frequently underestimated the
power of nationalism. A peculiar combination of economism
and illusions of linear progress (inherited from the
Enlightenment) led to the wrong belief that nationalism would
inevitably and quickly decline. The Second International in
particular believed that nationalism belonged to the past, and
Karl Kautsky dreamed of a socialist future without nations
and with one single language: 'In a painless way, the nations
will fuse with each other, more or less in the same fashion as
the Romansh inhabitants of the Grisons canton in
Switzerland, who, insensibly and without resistance, are slowly
germanising themselves as they discover that it is more advan-
tageous to speak a language that everybody understands in a
vast area rather than a language that is only spoken in a few
valleys.'[6] Obviously, equipped with such ideas, Marxists were
little prepared to confront the fantastic upsurge of nationalism
after August 1914, which took over the labour movement and
led to 'Sacred Unity in Defence of the Fatherland' – and to the
mutual slaughter of the workers of all countries. Kautsky
himself rallied to the 'national defence' of imperial Germany,
arguing that the Socialist International was an instrument
suited only for peacetime and had to be put gently aside
during the war.

The first condition for an effective confrontation with nationalism is therefore to give up illusions about linear progress, that is, naive expectations of peaceful evolution and of a gradual 'withering way' of nationalism and national wars, thanks to the modernisation and democratisation of industrial societies, the internationalisation of productive forces, etc.

How can one explain the incredible force of nationalism in the course of twentieth-century history? A first answer would be the classic Marxist argument: nationalism is a bourgeois ideology and its power over the popular masses is one of the main forms taken by the ideological domination of the bourgeoisie in capitalist societies. This analysis is not wrong, but insufficient to explain the power of attraction of nationalism, sometimes over significant sections of the labour movement. Other causes have to be taken into consideration.

First, concrete material and economic conditions: competition among workers of different nations (or states), resulting from the very nature of capitalism. It is a question of short-term interests – for instance, to prevent the entrance of foreign commodities which can provoke unemployment – but their real weight can blind competing workers to their common historical interest in abolishing exploitation. This, incidentally, also happens inside one single nation, when unemployed workers volunteer to replace striking ones. Marx himself recognised in the *Manifesto* that the competition among workers constantly threatens to divide and destroy their common organisation.

Second, irrational tendencies, similar in chauvinist nationalism, religious fanaticism, racism and fascism: a complex psychic phenomenon, which still has to be studied. Wilhelm Reich's work on the mass psychology of fascism, Erich Fromm's on 'escape from freedom' and Theodor Adorno's on the authoritarian personality are among the first important contributions to an explanation. Nationalism is by its very nature an irrationalist ideology: it cannot legitimate the privilege of one nation over the others with any rational criteria – since substantive (that is, not purely instrumental) rationality is always tendentially universal. It must therefore appeal to non-rational myths like the divine mission attributed to the nation, the innate and eternal superiority of a people, the right to occupy a larger geographical *Lebensraum,* etc. However, it may also make use of pseudo-rational and pseudo-scientific forms of legitimation, such as geopolitics or racial anthropology. Often it does not correspond to any deep historical and cultural unity, being just the official ideology of more or less artificial states, whose borders are the accidental product of colonisation and/or decolonisation (in Africa and Latin America for instance).

But there is another reason for the upsurge of nationalism, which has to be taken very seriously by Marxists and socialists: the struggle for liberation of oppressed or colonised nations. Although Marxism is as such opposed to nationalist ideology, it must very clearly distinguish between *the nationalism of the oppressors and the nationalism of the oppressed.* It has to support all struggles for national liberation or for oppressed nations' right to self-determination, even if their ideology (or the ideology of their leaders) is nationalist. Of course, Marxist internationalists taking part in a movement for national liberation should keep their independence and try to persuade the exploited popular masses of the need to develop the struggle (in an uninterrupted way) beyond national aims, towards a revolutionary socialist transformation. But they cannot ignore or underrate the significance of the popular demand for national self-determination.

The reason for this is not only that socialists are opposed to *all forms of oppression* (national, racial, sexual or class) but also because there is a *dialectical relationship* between internationalism and national rights. Socialist internationalism cannot develop without recognition by the socialist movement of the equal rights of all nations. In the same way as the unity and solidarity of the workers of one and the same nation cannot be established except on an egalitarian basis – without any distinctions or privileges based on occupation, religion, race, sex or branch of production – internationalist unity of the exploited can only be built on the recognition of the national rights and in particular the right to self-determination for all people.

When Lenin insisted that the Russian Social Democratic Workers Party should recognise Poland's right to self-determination – the right of the Polish people to decide for themselves if they wanted to establish a *separate state* or not – he did it not only because the struggle of the Polish nation against tsarism was historically progressive (the argument used by Marx and Engels) but above all because it was a pre-condition for the establishment of an internationalist alliance between Russian and Polish workers. Recognition of national rights is an essential condition for international solidarity, in so far as it permits the dissolution of suspicions, hatreds and fears which set nations against each other and nourish chauvinism. As Lenin wrote, without the right to divorce – to have a separate state – there can be no truly free marriage – unity or federation among nations. Unfortunately, the policy of the Bolshevik government (including Lenin) after October 1917 did not always correspond to this principle: for example, witness the invasion of Poland in 1920 and the occupation of Georgia in 1921.

By making the capital distinction between nationalism of the oppressed and of the oppressor, socialist internationalists do not have to adhere to the former. But they perceive its contradictory nature: its emancipatory dimension as a rebellion against unjust oppression and its limits as a particularistic ideology. It is therefore logical that all truly social revolutionary movements in an oppressed nation necessarily put national liberation at the centre of their struggle, while linking it to the social emancipation from capitalist exploitation – Nicaragua is a major recent example – while in the imperialist metropolis it is the rejection of nationalism which is at the heart of all radical confrontation with the established order, from the anti-war movement in the US to the French in May 1968 (whose main slogan was 'les frontières on s'en fout!' – 'Frontiers, the hell with them!').

This being said, it should be stressed that the distinction between the two kinds of nationalism is a *relative* and not an absolute one. First, because yesterday's oppressed very easily become today's oppressors: there is no lack of historical evidence for this in our own times. Second, because the nationalist ideology (or movement) of oppressed nations has often a double cutting edge: liberating against their oppressors, but oppressive towards their own national minorities. And third, because one can find in both forms of nationalism elements of chauvinism, global rejection of the 'other' and (sometimes) racism.

Lenin was probably the 'classic' Marxist thinker who best understood the dialectics between internationalism and national rights. However, in certain passages of his writings he presents the democratic rights of the nations as a *part* which has to be subordinated to the *whole* which is the world democratic and socialist movement. This formulation seems to me dangerous and somewhat mechanistic. If socialist revolution is the self-emancipation of the proletariat – in alliance with all the other exploited and oppressed social groups – it is intimately linked with the democratic self-determination of the nation. A people on whom 'socialism' was imposed from outside, against its will, would only know a caricature of socialism, inevitably doomed to bureaucratic degeneration. (Many Eastern European countries illustrate this rule!) In my opinion it would be more adequate – and corresponding better to the spirit of most of Lenin's writings on the national question – to conceive the socialist revolution and the international fraternity of the proletariat as Marxists' *aim* and national self-determination as a *necessary means* for implementing it. Means and ends are dialectically linked, in such a way that the subordination of the national dimension to internationalism excludes the possibility of 'sacrificing' the former to the latter.

Beyond Nations?

If socialist internationalism is opposed to nationalist ideology, this does not at all mean that it rejects nations' historical and cultural traditions. In the same way as internationalist movements in each country have to speak the national language, they have also to speak the language of national history and culture; particularly, of course, when this culture is being oppressed. As Lenin acknowledged, each culture and each national history contain democratic, progressive, revolutionary elements which have to be incorporated by the socialist culture of the labour movement, and reactionary, chauvinistic and obscurantist elements which have to be uncompromisingly fought. Internationalists' task is to fuse the historical and cultural heritage of the world socialist movement with the culture and the tradition of their people, in its radical and subversive dimension – often deformed by bourgeois ideology or hidden and buried by the official culture of the ruling classes. In the same way as Marxists must take into consideration, in their revolutionary struggle, the decisive importance of the national specificity of their social formation, in their ideological struggle they cannot ignore the national peculiarity of their own culture and history. This is what the Frente Sandinista de Liberación Nacional (FSLN) did in Nicaragua, linking Marxism with Sandino's heritage, a radical tradition alive in the collective memory of the Nicaraguan people. A similar process took place in Cuba with the democratic and anti-imperialist tradition represented by José Marti and in South America with the Indian rebellious past embodied by Tupac-Amaru.

If socialism, in the Marxian sense – a classless and stateless society – can exist only on a world scale, what would be the place of nations in a future 'Socialist Mother Earth'? This is not a purely utopian and irrelevant question, since the internationalist nature of the ultimate revolutionary socialist aim should inspire, to a certain extent at least, present forms of struggle. For historical materialism, the nation-state is not an eternal category: it is not the result of 'human nature' nor of any biological law of nature (a thesis advocated by certain ultra-reactionary 'sociobiologists' who pretend to deduce the nation from the 'territorial principle' of certain animal species). It did not always exist in the past and nothing forces one to believe that it will always exist in the future. In short, it is a historical product and can be historically superseded.

The necessity of some form of structured (or 'institutional') *organisation* is a universal need of all civilised human societies. This organisation can just as well take national forms as infranational (clans, tribes) or supranational ones (religious civilisations). Medieval Europe was a characteristic example of a social and political organisation combining local structures which were 'pre-national' (fiefs, principalities, etc.) and universalistic structures which were 'trans-national' (the Holy Roman Empire, the Church). The modern nation-state emerged in the fourteenth and fifteenth centuries – with the rise of capitalism and the formation of the national market – precisely through the destruction/decomposition of these two non-national structures.

There is therefore no *a priori* reason to deny the possibility in the future of a new supranational organisation of human society, a World Socialist Republic, which, unifying economically and politically the human species, would reduce the nation essentially to its cultural dimension. The universal culture which would arise in such a framework would peacefully co-exist with the rich multiplicity of the national cultures.

This issue has been quite controversial in twentieth-century Marxism. One can find basically two tendencies: 1. Those who favoured (or considered inevitable) the future assimilation of all nations in a universal common socialist culture: Kautsky, Lenin, Stalin, Pannekoek, Strasser. Kautsky's theory of the single international language is a coherent expression of this position. 2. Those who believed in the free development of all national cultures in an integrated universal community: Bauer, Trotsky and Luxemburg. For instance, Trotsky wrote in a 1915 essay: 'The nation is an active and permanent factor of human culture. And in a socialist regime the nation, liberated from the chains of political and economic dependence, will be called to play a fundamental role in historical development.'[7] A third position, 'national neutrality', is implicitly sketched by Vladimir Medem, the leader of the Jewish Bund: it is impossible to predict whether future historical development will or not lead to the assimilation of the Jewish nation. In any case, Marxists should neither prevent nor stimulate this process of assimilation, but remain neutral.[8] If one generalises this position to all national cultures (which Medem did not) one would have an original and new conception of the problem.[9]

In any case, the most important, from a socialist, revolutionary and *democratic* viewpoint, is that no internationalist politics can be based on the denial, repression, neglect or limitation of the national right to self-determination and self-development.

CHAPTER 6

Why Nationalism?

The burning problems of our times – such as the growing gap between the South and the North, the need for general disarmament, the world capitalist crisis, the threat of ecological catastrophe – are obviously of an international character. They can hardly be solved on a local, regional or national scale. However, at the same time as the world economy is becoming more and more unified by multinational capitalism, a spectacular tide of nationalism is rising, in Europe and on a world scale, submerging everything in its way.

While some national movements are emancipatory and progressive, nationalism is very often a 'false solution' to the economic, social, political and ecological challenges of our times. Why then has it become so popular in so many countries and areas of the world?

There is no easy explanation for this upsurge, but it could be helpful to compare it with the parallel revival of religious feelings. The crisis of both existing models of (instrumental) rationality – capitalist accumulation and bureaucratic productivism – favours the development of non-rational (sometimes irrational) reactions such as religion and nationalism. Of course, both phenomena can also take progressive forms – as in national liberation movements or in liberation theology – but the regressive tendencies (nationalist and/or religious intolerance) are quite formidable.

In many countries of the world, religion tends to merge with nationalism, infusing it with greater power of attraction and an aura of 'sacredness': this is true of Catholicism in Poland and Croatia (as well as, in a different context, Ireland), of Eastern Orthodoxy in Serbia and Russia, of conservative evangelism in the US, of certain forms of Jewish orthodoxy in Israel, of Islam in Libya and Iran. In other cases, religion and nationalism are competing rivals or even forces in open conflict, as it is the case with Islamic fundamentalism and Arab nationalism in North Africa and the Middle East.

In any case, nationalism has its own roots and does not depend necessarily on religion in order to expand. How do we explain its present rise? One could perhaps consider the nationalist wave as a sort of reaction to the growing internationalisation of the economy and (to a certain extent) of culture, a struggle against the threat of homogenisation. It could also be understood as a compensatory movement, trying to counterbalance the decline of economic independence by reinforcing (sometimes in monstrous proportions) ethical, political and cultural aspects of national identity.

A similar (but different) hypothesis was suggested by Theodor Adorno at a conference in 1966 (on 'Education after Auschwitz'): if nationalism is so aggressive 'it is because in the era of international communication and supra-national blocs, it cannot really believe in itself, and has no choice but to become outrageously excessive, if it wants to persuade both itself and others of its substantive character'.[1] Of course, the argument applies to a much greater degree to the situation in Europe in the 1990s than in the 1960s.

However, this and other general interpretations, although useful, cannot quite explain the extraordinary diversity of the phenomenon, which takes very different forms in different parts of the world. One has therefore to examine the *specific nature of nationalism in each of its multiple contexts,* in order to be able to understand its moving forces.

Eastern Europe

Let us begin with *the region* where this new nationalist tide is particularly visible: Eastern Europe and the former USSR. An intelligent observer of Eastern European politics has summarised the events in this part of the world remarkably well:

The last remnants of solidarity between the nonemancipated nationalities in the 'belt of mixed populations' evaporated with the disappearance of a central despotic bureaucracy which had also served to gather together and divert from each other the diffuse hatreds and conflicting national claims. Now everybody was against everybody else, and most of all against their closest neighbours – the Slovaks against the Czechs, the Croats against the Serbs, the Ukrainians against the Poles.

The most astonishing thing in this analysis is that it was *not* written a few weeks ago. It is a passage from the well-known book of Hannah Arendt on the origins of totalitarianism, published in 1951, which describes 'the atmosphere of disintegration' in Eastern Europe during the 1920s, after the liquidation of the Austro-Hungarian monarchy and the tsarist empire – the two 'despotic bureaucracies' referred to in the above quotation.[2]

Incidentally, a similar assessment can also be found in Rosa Luxemburg's notes on war and nationalism from 1918: 'Nationalism is at the moment a trump. From all sides nations and semi-nations appear and claim their right to form a State ... At the nationalist Brocken it is now the time of the Walpurgis night.'[3]

In other words: we have been drawn, in a large part of Europe, *70 years back*.

Let there be no misunderstanding: there is nothing regressive – on the contrary – when (today, as in 1920) multinational empires, which had become true 'prisons of peoples', crumble and the oppressed nations recover their liberty. To that extent, there is undeniably a *democratic moment* in the national revival which has taken place since 1989 in Eastern Europe and the former USSR. Socialists and democrats could only rejoice when Soviet tanks left East Germany, Poland and Hungary and the troops of the KGB quit the Baltic countries, leaving these people to decide their future for themselves and freely choose unity, separation or federation.

Unfortunately, not everything is so pleasant in this picture: the best and the worst are inseparably mixed in these national movements. The best: the democratic awakening of spoliated nations, the rediscovery of their language and culture, the aspiration for freedom and popular sovereignty. The worst: the awakening of chauvinistic nationalisms, of expansionism, of intolerance, of xenophobia; the resurrection of old national quarrels, hatred against the 'hereditary enemy', the growth of authoritarian tendencies, leading to the oppression of one's own national minorities; and finally, the upsurge of fascist, semi-fascist and racist forms of nationalism, in Russia ('Pamiat'), Romania, Slovakia, Croatia (Neo-Ustashe), Serbia (Neo-Chetniks), the former GDR (Neo-Nazis) and elsewhere as well. The eternal scapegoats of the past – Jews and Gypsies – are again being selected as responsible for all the evils of society.

Paradoxically, this negative and sinister aspect, this 'return of the repressed', this resurrection of ancient national vendettas appears nowhere in a more brutal and absurd form than in Yugoslavia – the only one of the so-called 'socialist' countries in Eastern Europe which had been able to escape from the control of Moscow and to establish a relatively egalitarian federation between its component nations. Anti-fascist solidarity among the various nationalities, rooted in the Communist Partisan fight of the Second World War, left the stage, to be replaced by a savage *bella omnia contra omnes*.

Of course, one can explain this paradox by several and complex economic, cultural, political, religious and historical causes – without forgetting the heavy responsibility of the Serbian Stalino-nationalist regime of Milosevic, who opened, with his policy of oppression against Kosovo's Albanians, the Pandora's box of nationalisms in the country.[4] Nevertheless, there remains an irreducible kernel of pure irrationality in this explosion of hatred against the 'other', whose most dreadful expression was the policy of 'ethnic cleansing' implemented by Serb nationalist forces in Bosnia-Hercegovina.

Russia's war against Chechenya was another example of the savagery unleashed by post-Soviet nationalism. It is impossible to predict, for the moment, if the 'Yugoslav paradigm' is going to be followed by others and if present conflicts such as those between Slovaks and Czechs, Hungarians and Romanians, Moldavians and Russians, Azeris and Armenians, Georgians and Ossetians, and Russians and Ukrainians will or will not take the form of a general confrontation; and if the dissolution of the former USSR will or will not lead to national wars (with nuclear arms?) that would make the conflict in Yugoslavia look like a small incident. Anything can happen, and unfortunately the worst is a distinct possibility.

The reasons for this nationalist explosion, which is shaking practically the whole former 'socialist bloc', are, among others, the following:

1. The rebellion against decades of national discrimination and 'Great Russian' hegemonism. This is the most obvious motive behind national movements, both in the former USSR and in its 'satellites'. There is no doubt that the annexation of the Baltic states during the Second World War, and the invasion of Hungary in 1956 and Czechoslovakia in 1968, left a very deep imprint in the national consciousness of these countries. Once the iron lid of Soviet occupation was lifted, it is understandable that a vast nationalist upsurge would take place. But this, however, does not apply to Yugoslavia, an independent state which had liberated itself from Soviet hegemony in 1948.

2. According to the Czech historian Miroslav Hroch, 'where an old regime disintegrates, where old social relations have become unstable, amid the rise of general insecurity, belonging to a common language and culture may become the only certainty in society'.[5]

This helps one to understand the parallel between present events and those of the 1920s, after the disintegration of the traditional empires in Central and Eastern Europe.

3. The collapse of socialist ideas, values and images (including the idea of 'proletarian internationalism'), as well as of working-class culture, discredited by so many years of bureaucratic manipulation and identified by very broad masses as the official doctrine of the 'old regime'. Politics, like nature, detests a vacuum. No other rival political ideology had such a powerful tradition and such ancient roots in popular culture as nationalism – often combined, as we have seen, with religion. Liberal individualism of the Western kind, while attractive to the intelligentsia and the rising new class of businessmen, had little appeal to the broad mass of the population.

4. The desire of relatively advanced nations, regions or republics to cut loose from poorer and relatively backward areas, in order to keep their own resources for themselves and to join, as quickly as possible, the Western European market.

This applies particularly to Slovenia and Croatia, to the Baltic republics and in general to the western parts of the former USSR (in relation to the Asiatic ones). A similar phenomenon, by the way, can also be found in northern Italy (the rise of the so-called Lombard Leagues).

To these main explanations, one has to add the manipulation of nationalist feelings by neo-Stalinist or neo-liberal elites trying to keep (or to win back) their power: Azerbaijan, Russia, Serbia and Croatia are good examples of this process.

What Use Is Marxism?

Of what help, in so chaotic a situation, confronted with such a confused maelstrom of territorial conflicts, historical claims, chauvinist exclusions and liberating uprisings, can the analytic and political instruments of Marxism be? Marxism has the great advantage of a critical/rational, as well as humanist/universal, standpoint. But it will remain disarmed in confronting present developments, if it is not able to get rid of certain myths and illusions which are part of its own tradition.

Among the myths, there is one which is particularly obnoxious: the idea of a 'scientific' and 'objective' definition of the nation. Thanks to Stalin, this dogma wrought havoc in four continents, transforming theory into a true Procrustean bed, imposed by decree of the Political Bureau (charged with verifying if this or that nation measured up to the 'objective' criteria or not).

Happily, most Marxists dealing today with the national question have understood quite well that nations cannot be defined in purely objective terms (such as territory, language or economic unit) – even if these are far from being irrelevant – but that they are *imagined communities* (Benedict Anderson), *cultural creations* (Eric Hobsbawm). As early as 1939 Trotsky insisted, in a discussion with C.L.R James about African-Americans, that 'on this matter an abstract criterion is not decisive, but the historical consciousness, the feelings and impulses of a group are more important'.[6]

As far as illusions are concerned, there is one which can be found in Marx himself and which haunts the reflections of the best Marxists from Rosa Luxemburg up to our own day: the imminent decline of nationalism and of the nation-state, made anachronistic by the internationalisation of the economy.

An attenuated version of this hypothesis can still be found in 1988, on the eve of the most formidable nationalist wave in Europe since the Second World War. In his, otherwise excellent, book on nations and nationalism since 1780, Hobsbawm risked the following diagnosis: 'while nobody can possibly deny the growing and sometimes dramatic, impact of nationalist, or ethnic politics, there is one major aspect in which the phenomenon today is functionally different from the "nationalism" and the "nations" of 19th- and earlier 20th-century history. It is no longer a major vector of historical development'. In his opinion, 'the declining historical significance of nationalism is today concealed ... by the visible spread of ethnic/linguistic agitation'. In other words, 'in spite of its evident prominence nationalism is historically less important. It is no longer, as it were, a global political programme, as it may be said to have been in the nineteenth and earlier twentieth centuries. It is at most a complicating factor, or a catalyst for other developments.'[7]

One would like to subscribe to this optimistic view of things (from the standpoint of internationalist socialism), but one can hardly avoid the impression that the great historian is taking his desires for reality. One does not need to sympathise with nationalist ideologies in order to take into account their growing influence in Europe. It is difficult to predict what is going to happen during the next century, but now, and in the coming years, it is impossible to consider the role of nationalism in Europe (and elsewhere) as a minor or secondary factor.

Hobsbawm is more to the point when he shows the inadequacy of nationalist 'solutions', particularly in Eastern Europe. Unlike nationalists, Marxists are convinced that national independence – although necessary, in many cases – is far from sufficient to solve the basic economic, social, ecological or political problems confronting the population – particularly if we consider the new kind of economic (and therefore also political) dependence of the recently emancipated nations on Western finance.

Western Europe

Western European liberals often consider this Eastern nationalist explosion – and its xenophobic manifestations – as the
product of 'underdevelopment', of primitive semi-agrarian
societies, of populations having lived too long under
'communism' and lacking democratic experience. Some even
claim that nationalism is only a plot of ex-communists (as in
Serbia, Bulgaria or Azerbaijan) to keep power. Western
Europe is presented as a harmonious world, well beyond such
irrational passions. Reconciled, the nations of this democratic
and modern part of the continent are quickly moving towards
their integration in a united European Community.

This idyllic image does not quite correspond to reality. It is
an illusion, if not a mystification, to claim that Western Europe
is now 'beyond nationalism' or that it has, as Ernst Gellner
recently wrote, achieved 'Stage Five' in the history of European
nationalism, a 'relatively benign condition' in which 'economic
and cultural convergence jointly diminish ethnic hostilities'.[8]

National conflicts, nationalist feelings and nationalist
movements exist in Western Europe as well, and are growing.
They belong basically to two very different species:

1. The (usually progressive) movements for the rights of
national minorities and/or *oppressed nations*. The Basque and
Irish are only the (explosive) tip of the iceberg, which includes
Catalans and Galicians, Scots and Welsh, Corsicans, Greek
Cypriots and several others.[9]

2. *Xenophobic and racist nationalism,* directed not so much
against the old 'enemy from outside' (other European nations)
but against the 'enemy within': immigrant workers of Arab,
African, Turkish, Kurdish or Eastern European origin (as well
as, often, Jewish or Gypsy minorities). The political expression
of this development is the surprising rise of nationalist parties
and movements of semi-fascist, fascist or even Nazi character
(such as in France, Austria, Belgium and Germany) – repres-
enting already 7 million voters in the European Union! – as
well as murderous attacks by skinheads and other racist gangs.
In Germany alone in 1991, there were more than 1200 attacks
by racist thugs against foreign immigrants (compared with 270
in 1990).[10]

It is true that racism is not identical to nationalism. But as Adorno already emphasised at the above-mentioned conference in 1966, 'the awakening of nationalism is the most favourable climate' for an upsurge of racism and intolerance.[11] In its most radical and extreme forms, nationalism often turns into racism, by trying to ground national supremacy on pseudo-biological criteria.

The main targets of Western European xenophobic nationalism were until recently immigrants from the South (particularly Africa and Asia). The next victims will be – or are already, mainly in Germany – the unfortunate immigrants from Eastern Europe, expelled from their countries by national conflicts or by the economic catastrophe resulting from the brutal introduction of a market economy. After the Arab, the African or the Turk, it is now the turn of the Pole, the Romanian or the Albanian to become the scapegoat for Western racist/nationalists.

Mainstream Western European parties refuse to endorse racism, but they share a sort of 'Western nationalism' which leads to denying democratic rights (for example, to vote and be elected) to immigrant workers and to the closure, as tightly as possible, of EU borders to non-Western immigrants. Could it be that one day the European Union will rebuild the Berlin Wall a little further to the east and re-establish the barriers of electrified barbed wire of the old 'Iron Curtain', this time on the western side of the border?

As a matter of fact, the presence of immigrants is only a pretext. They constitute no more than 2 per cent of the European Union's population; moreover, they were already there 15 or 20 years ago, without provoking the same reactions. Why has this xenophobic wave begun *now*?

The economic crisis, unemployment and the degradation of living conditions in popular neighbourhoods are certainly among the main factors. But there is something deeper taking place in the political culture of some popular layers. As in Eastern Europe, but in a different way, the decline of socialist and class values, so long identified with the USSR and the communist parties, is making room for nationalism/racism. From this standpoint, the rise of nationalist values has common roots in both parts of Europe.

To this one has to add, in the West, disappointment with the social-democratic management of the crisis, increasingly undistinguishable (with the exception of a few details) from the neo-liberal one. The failure of social-democratic governments (or coalitions including such parties) to confront growing social inequalities, their adoption of the conventional (bourgeois) economic wisdom and their involvement in various corruption scandals (for example, in France and Italy) have paved the way for all sorts of xenophobic 'populist' movements. Thanks to the weakening of socialist culture, capitalism appears more and more as a 'natural' system, as the only possible horizon, as the necessary form of production and exchange. As a result, economic and social problems like unemployment, poverty or urban insecurity are no longer attributed by significant sections of the population to the dysfunctions of capitalism, but to the presence of immigrants and other 'foreigners'.

The Ex-Third World

Progressive and reactionary forms of nationalism can also be found in the so-called Third World (a term which has lost any meaning, since there is no longer any 'Second World'), that is, in the dependent periphery of the imperialist world system.

Several important emancipatory and progressive national liberation movements can be found today in Africa, Asia and the Middle East. But it should be emphasised that most of these movements – such as those in Kurdistan, Palestine, East Timor and southern Sudan – are not directly opposed to Western imperialism as such but rather to local forms of national oppression. With the exception of the wave of popular protest in the Arab world against the Gulf War, anti-colonial and anti-imperialist nationalism seems to have lost much of its influence, to the benefit of basically reactionary and/or xeno-phobic movements like Islamic fundamentalism, ethno-linguistic and religious communalism (India, Sri Linka) and tribalism – shown most horrifyingly in the genocide of as many as a million Tutsi in Rwanda in 1994.

Contradictory forms of nationalism co-exist in Latin-America as well.[12] The classic example of reactionary nationalism is the 'patriotic' ideology of military regimes – as in Argentina, Brazil or Chile in the 1970s and 1980 – usually directed against the ghost of 'international communism' and its Latin American 'subversive agents'. In the name of the 'doctrine of national security', every social protest, every leftist movement was denounced as being 'of foreign inspiration' or based on 'exotic doctrines alien to our national tradition'. This conservative brand of Cold War nationalism made extensive use of national symbols (the flag, the national anthem) and patriotic rhetoric, but it accepted US hegemony ('the American leadership of the Free World') without hesitation. It may have referred to geopolitics in order to claim a sub-imperialist role of regional hegemony – like the Brazilian military during the 1970s – but this ambition very seldom led to an open conflict with rival Western powers, as in the Argentinian war with Britain over the Malvinas/Falkland islands.

Middle-class populist nationalism, which had its peak during the 1940s and 1950s (Peronism in Argentina, the Peruvian APRA, 'Getulismo' in Brazil, etc.) is in decline and has come to terms with foreign capital. The most obvious example is the Peronist government in Argentina (President Menem), which systematically broke all links with the nationalist tradition of the movement and followed very strictly the instructions of the IMF. In some cases, like Mexico, the crisis of the governmental populist movement (the PRI, Institutional Revolutionary Party) has led to a split and the formation of a new party. The Mexican PRD (Revolutionary Democratic Party), led by Cuauhtémoc Cárdenas – the son of former president Lázaro Cárdenas, who expropriated the US oil companies in Mexico during the 1930s – aims at a renewal of the nationalist and anti-imperialist tradition of the Mexican Revolution.

Revolutions in Latin America always had simultaneously a *social* and a *national* content. This applied not only to the Mexican Revolution of 1910–11 or the Bolivian Revolution of 1953, but also to the more radical revolutions (aiming at a socialist transformation) in Cuba (1959–61) and Nicaragua (1979). Fidel Castro and his followers were inspired by the struggle and the ideas of José Marti, the Jacobin, nationalist and anti-imperialist leader of the insurrection against Spanish colonialism; and the the fighters of the FSLN (Frente Sandinista de Liberáción Nacional) in Nicaragua considered themselves heirs to Augusto Sandino's war of national liberation against the US marines (1927–32). The struggle for national independence and sovereignty, in confrontation with aggressive US imperial policies, was a decisive component of the Cuban and Nicaraguan revolutionary movements and of their popular support.

Today, the fight against foreign debt and IMF policies has been the main focus of progressive national feelings and anti-imperialist mobilisations in Latin America, taking the form of rallies, strikes, protests and even mass riots. Thanks to the heavy requirements of (strictly speaking impossible) debt repayment, the IMF and the World Bank exert such direct control (without precedent since the end of Spanish colonisation in the nineteenth century!) over the economic and social policies of these countries that their independence is often reduced to a fiction. The 'advisers' and 'experts' of the international financial institutions dictate to Latin American governments their rate of inflation, their budgetary cuts in education and health, their wages policy and their tax structure. The popular struggle against such outrageous forms of dependency, and against the repayment of the foreign debt, is not only a 'nationalist', but also an *anti-systemic* (to use Immanuel Wallerstein's useful concept) movement, by its opposition to the logic of world capitalist finance. It has also a 'class' component, by its conflict with the local rulers – eager to comply with the policies of the IMF and of the foreign banks.

It is not surprising that in some countries, like Brazil, Bolivia or Peru, it is the labour movements, unions and leftist parties that lead the fight against the repayment of the foreign debt: national and social liberation are intimately linked in the consciousness of the most active sections of the movement. Lula, the leader of the Brazilian Partido dos Trabalhadores (Workers Party) – who gained 47 per cent of the vote in the 1989 presidential elections – called for an immediate suspension of payment and the establishment of a public enquiry on the debt, in order to find out what happened to the money borrowed (mainly by the military regime which ruled the country from 1964 to 1985). He also called for a common initiative of the indebted countries, since none of them is strong enough to confront the creditors alone.

How far can a single country – even a powerful one like Brazil or Mexico – go in rejecting the dictatorship of the World Bank and breaking the yoke of imperialist domination? Can Latin American unity, under popular leadership, constitute an alternative to US plans for economic integration? How to achieve national and social liberation in an underdeveloped country without the economic or military support of an industrial power like the USSR? How important are the contradictions between Europe, Japan and the US, and could they be exploited by liberated peripheral countries?

These and similar questions – which cannot be easily answered – are being debated among progressive, socialist and anti-imperialist forces, in Latin America and elsewhere in the ex-Third World. They show that national liberation is still a key issue at the periphery of the system, but also that purely nationalist solutions are of limited value: the need for an internationalist strategy is perhaps better perceived now than in the past.

The example of Cuba seems to show that an independent country can, at least for a limited amount of time, survive in confrontation with a US blockade, a boycott by the world financial institutions and no support from the former USSR. But in the longer run, the future of Cuba will depend on developments in the other parts of Latin America.

In recent years, the various socialist, nationalist and anti-imperialist forces in Latin America – including, among others, the Brazilian PT, the Nicaraguan FSLN, the Salvadoran FMLN (Farabundo Marti National Liberation Front), the Mexican PRD and the Cuban Communist Party – feeling the need of an international (or at least regional) coordination, have associated themselves in a united front, called the São Paulo Forum, which meets yearly and discusses common perspectives. At the first conference of the Forum, in 1990, a document was adopted, which presented the broad outlines of a common strategy for national liberation in Latin America. First of all, it rejected the proposal for 'American integration' proposed by US President Bush, denouncing it as an attempt to 'completely open our national economies to the unfair and unequal competition of the imperialist economic apparatus, submitting entirely to its hegemony and destroying our productive structures, by integrating us into a free-trade zone hegemonised and organised by US interests'. The document counterposes to this proposal for integration under imperialist domination 'a new concept of continental unity and integration', based on the sovereignty and self-determination of Latin America, the recovery of its historical and cultural identity and the internationalist solidarity of its peoples.

> This presupposes the defense of the Latin American patrimony, an end to the flight and export of the continent's capital, a common and united policy towards the scourge of an unpayable foreign debt, and the adoption of economic policies in the service of the majority, capable of alleviating the poverty in which millions of Latin Americans live.[13]

Along with anti-imperialist nationalism, a different sort of emancipatory nationalism has been developing in Latin America in recent years: the movement of the indigenous nations for their rights. The debate around the quincentennial of Columbus's arrival in the Americas and the Nobel Prize granted to Rigoberta Menchú have given greater visibility to the indigenous struggle for the defence of their communities, their land and their national culture against the oppression of the ruling oligarchies (usually of Spanish descent).

These Indian movements, associations or political parties (like the Tupac Katari Movement in Bolivia) – which usually are not limited to one ethnic group (Quechuas, Aymaras, Mayas) but unite all the Indian communities in each country – develop a thorough criticism of Western civilisation and its values (private property, individualism, commodity production) in the name of pre-capitalist (and pre-Columbian) indigenous traditions and their communitarian culture. Their struggle has at one and the same time a national, social and ecological character.

While some organisations have a stronger ethnic component and call for the restoration of the old Indian nations and empires, most of those movements fight for the recognition of the national and cultural rights of the indigenous peoples in coalition with other oppressed groups and classes. One example of this was the continent-wide movement in 1992 against the official celebrations of the quincentennial, called 'Five Hundred Years of Indian, Black and Popular Resistance', which had as one of its main aims solidarity with the struggles of indigenous peoples. Of course, there are very great differences between the indigenous nations of countries like Guatemala, Peru and Bolivia, where they constitute the majority of the population, and the small surviving tribes of the Amazonian area. While in the former case the national struggle is intimately linked to the social one and to the agrarian question (the struggle for land), in the latter case it is rather a matter of protection against the ethnocidal logic of 'civilisation'.

The resistance of trade unionists, ecologists and Indian tribes against the destructive development of agribusiness may lead to common action, as happened in the Brazilian Amazon region with the constitution of a Confederation of the Rain Forest Peoples by initiative of the well-known trade union and ecological leader Chico Mendes (later killed by landowners).

Finally, there is a third form of progressive nationalism in Latin America (and the US as well): black nationalism, which is particularly important in the Caribbean countries. Its historical roots can be found in the slave rebellions and in particular in the Haitian Revolution of 1791 led by Toussaint L'Ouverture and the Black Jacobins. In a country like Brazil, where the majority of the population is black or coloured, there have also been slave revolts (like the Quilombo dos Palmares, a community of rebel slaves during the eighteenth century). In our time, the main form of Brazilian black cultural resistance is religious, through the development of Umbanda, a syncretic cult composed of African and Christian elements.

Universalism True and False

What should be the attitude of Marxists in relation to national conflicts? Marxism is opposed to nationalist ideology, but it does not ignore the importance and legitimacy of democratic national rights.

This is why, during conflicts between Western imperial powers and dependent countries of Asia, Africa or Latin America, Marxists usually defend the rights of the peripheral nations and struggle against all forms of imperial aggression (whatever their 'democratic' or 'juridical' cover). But this does *not* mean that they should give any kind of support to reactionary military, religious or nationalist dictators in the Third World, like General Videla, Ayatollah Khomeini, Saddam Hussein or General Noriega.

As an internationalist worldview, Marxism – as distinguished from its multiple national-bureaucratic counterfeits – has the advantage of a universalist and critical position, in contrast to the passions and intoxications of nationalist mythology. That is on the condition, however, that this universalism does not remain abstract, grounded on the simple negation of national particularity, but becomes a true 'concrete universal' (Hegel), able to incorporate, under the form of a dialectical *Aufhebung* ('sublation', transcendence) all the richness of the particular.

Thanks to the concept of *imperialism*, Marxism is able to avoid the pitfalls of the Eurocentric (or 'Western') false universalism, which claims to impose on all countries in the world (and particularly those on the periphery), under the cover of 'civilisation', the domination of the modern bourgeois industrial way of life: private property, market economy, unlimited economic expansion, productivism, utilitarianism, possessive individualism and instrumental rationality.

This does not mean that socialists ignore the universal value of certain achievements of European culture since 1789, such as democracy and human rights. It means only that they refuse the false dilemma between a pretend 'Western' universalism and narrow-minded worship of cultural differences.

For Marxism, the most important universal value is the liberation of human beings from all forms of oppression, domination, alienation and degradation. This is a utopian universality, in opposition to the *ideological* universalities which apologetically present the Western status quo as being the already-realised universal human culture, the end of history, the incarnation of the absolute spirit. Only a *critical* universality of this kind, looking towards an emancipated future, is able to overcome short-sighted nationalisms, narrow culturalisms and ethnocentrisms.

Starting from this premiss, how should Marxists react to the present European national conflicts or to Third World communal strife?

First of all, the Marxist distinction between the *nationalism of the oppressors* and of the *oppressed* is more than ever justified, and it operates like a precious compass to find one's bearings in the present tempest. But its use is made difficult by a well-known characteristic of modern nationalisms: each oppressed nation, as soon as it is liberated (or even before), considers it its most urgent task to exercise an analogous oppression over its own national minorities. Frequently, during the present inter-ethnic conflicts, each side persecutes the minority belonging to the rival nation, while manipulating its own nationals on the other side of the border (former Yugoslavia is a case in point).

We need, therefore, a universal criterion in order to untangle the web of the opposed and mutually exclusive claims. This criterion can only be that – common to socialists and democrats – of the right of self-determination (including separation) of each nation, meaning of each community which considers itself as such. Indifferent to the myths of blood and soil and not recognising any purely religious or historical claims over a given territory, this criterion has the immense advantage of referring itself only to the *universal principles of democracy and popular sovereignty,* and of taking into consideration only the concrete demographic realities of any inhabited space.

This principle does not prevent socialists from defending the option which seems to them the most desirable or the most progressive at a given historical moment: state separation (independence), federation or confederation. The essential point is that the nations and nationalities concerned should freely decide their own future. This rule – incorporated by Lenin into the Marxist lexicon – is more necessary than ever. But, again, its application to current national conflicts – particularly in Eastern Europe and the former USSR – is not always easy. In many cases the interpenetration of nationalities is such that any attempt to cut borders into this mosaic is fraught with perils. The dream of national homogeneity inside the state, which haunts almost all nationalisms, is a most dangerous perspective. As Hobsbawm observes, in a sober historical reminder:

> The logical implication of trying to create a continent neatly divided into coherent territorial states, each inhabited by a separate ethnically and linguistically homogeneous population, was the mass expulsion and extermination of minorities. Such was and is the murderous *reductio ad absurdum* of nationalism in its territorial version, although this was not fully demonstrated until the 1940s.[14]

Let us return to our initial paradox: at this strange nationalist *fin-de-siècle*, the most urgent problems have, more than ever, an international character. The search for a way out of the economic crisis of the former socialist bloc, the question of the Third World's debt and imminent ecological disaster – to mention only these three major examples – require planetary solutions. Capital's solutions are well known and perfectly organised on a world scale: inevitably, wherever they have been implemented, they have the same dual result: make the rich even richer and the poor even poorer.

What alternatives exist to the totalitarian grip of 'really existing' capitalism? The old pseudo-internationalism of the Stalinist Comintern, of the followers of various 'socialist fatherlands', is dead and buried. A new internationalist alternative of the oppressed and exploited is badly needed.

It is from the fusion between the international socialist, democratic and anti-imperialist tradition of the labour movement (still very much alive among revolutionaries of various tendencies such as radical trade unionists and left socialists) and the new universalist culture of social movements like ecology, feminism, anti-racism and Third World solidarity that the internationalism of tomorrow will rise. This tendency may be a minority now, but it is nevertheless the seed of a different future and the ultimate guarantee against barbarism.

CHAPTER 7

Twenty-first-century Internationalism

What happened to socialist internationalism in the twentieth century?

August 1914 brought a catastrophic breakdown of internationalism, when the great majority of the socialist labour movement (leadership as well as rank and file) was engulfed by the immense wave of nationalist (and chauvinist) hysteria, in the name of 'national defence'. However, this was not to be the end of internationalism, but the beginning of a *new* internationalist upsurge in the socialist movement, at first limited to small circles of revolutionaries or pacifists, and then, after October 1917, growing into an impressive mass movement: the Communist International. The existence of the Comintern, a world movement genuinely committed to proletarian internationalism (at least during its first years), is a powerful historical proof that the international solidarity of the exploited is not just a utopia, an abstract principle, but that in given circumstances it can have mass appeal among workers and other exploited social layers. In several key European and 'colonial' countries, the Third International soon rallied the majority of the organised labour movement, invalidating the conservative myth that the great masses of the working people cannot transcend nationalist ideology.

This is decisive evidence that internationalism – and revolutionary class consciousness in general – is an *objective possibility*, based on reality and its contradictions. Of course, its concrete implementation depends on historical circumstances and on a political battle of the revolutionary forces to win the people and liberate them from the blinkers of nationalism. In other words: Marxist internationalism – as well as the hope of revolution – is based not only on an objective analysis of world economy and world politics, but also on a historical wager; a wager on the rationality of the working people, on the capacity of the popular masses to understand, sooner or later, their objective historical interests.

However, this extraordinary upsurge of internationalist faith and action – without precedent in the past history of socialism – the incredible capital of internationalist energy and commitment represented by the Communist International was wasted by Stalinism. It channelled this energy in the service of bureaucratic nationalism, its state policy and its power strategy. Internationalism became the handmaid of Soviet diplomacy and the world communist movement an instrument to help build 'socialism in one country'. The most obvious example is the policy of the Comintern towards German Nazism, from 1928 until its dissolution in 1943: its strange turns and about-faces had little to do with the life-and-death interests of European workers and peoples, but were exclusively determined by changing Soviet diplomatic and military alliances.

Nevertheless, during the 1930s Europe saw *the* most impressive example of *internationalist practice*: the International Brigades in Spain and the general mobilisation in solidarity with the anti-fascist struggle during the Spanish Civil War. Tens of thousands of volunteers – communists, socialists, anarchists, Trotskyists, independent Marxists, radicalised liberals and anti-fascists of various tendencies – from dozens of nationalities came from all over the world in order to help the Spanish people in its desperate war against fascism. Thanks to Hitler and Mussolini's help to Franco (and the so-called 'non-interventionist' policy of the Western democracies) this war was lost, but the fight of the International Brigades – many of whose volunteers fell on the battle-field – remains one of the highest manifestations of internationalism in the twentieth century.

After (and also during) the Second World War nationalism became the dominant ideology again – even among the 'really existing socialist countries', who engaged in a process of nationalist confrontation (USSR vs. China) or war (China vs. Vietnam). What remained as 'internationalism' in the world communist movement after the dissolution of the Comintern was only blind fidelity to the Soviet Union and its leadership (now vanished). The only exceptions were small revolutionary tendencies, among them the Fourth International, who remained committed to the original internationalist aims of the Comintern, but their influence was limited. This decline in communist internationalism left an ideological void which very quickly was to be filled by nationalism.

While the old internationalism identified with the Soviet Union is dead, there are new forms of internationalist solidarity which are emerging in our times. The 1960s already produced a big and unexpected wave of internationalism among the younger generation, taking the form of anti-war movements, solidarity with Third World revolutions and the rejection of nationalist chauvinism. May 1968 saw hundreds of young French people chanting 'Nous sommes tous des juifs allemands' ('We are all German Jews'): a slogan which expressed this spontaneous and massive internationalist feeling.

Today a *new internationalist culture* is in the making. In the Third World it results from the convergence between a new Marxist Left – which rejects the disastrous Stalinist tradition of blind allegiance to a 'socialist fatherland' (USSR, China, Albania, etc.) – and Christian socialists linked to liberation theology. The catholic – in the sense of international – character of religion has entered, thanks to liberation theology, into a relationship of elective affinity with Marxist internationalism. Whatever the limits of their international outlook, Sandinismo in Nicaragua and the Brazilian Workers Party have been examples of this.

Among the new generation, this new internationalist culture in process of constitution is the product of various components, which combine and fuse with each other in various proportions. These can be enumerated as follows:

1. What remained from the older socialist tradition of proletarian and revolutionary internationalism – kept alive among left socialists, critical communists, anarchists and in such organisations as the Fourth International – and from the New Left culture of the 1960s.

2. Ecology, whose struggle to protect Nature and 'Mother Earth' from destructive 'progress', industrial waste and ecological disaster knows no borders and relates to a common interest of all humankind.

3. Anti-racism, a spontaneous movement of solidarity with the (African, Arab, Asian or Turkish) immigrant population, rejecting the nationalist/racist logic of exclusion. One of the most important issues raised by this movement (particularly in France) is the separation between nationality and citizenship: all inhabitants living in a country should be considered citizens (with the right of vote) independently of their nationality.

4. Feminism, which subverts the traditional patriarchal culture of aggressive nationalism, 'male' military virtues and 'heroic' patriotic violence. If there is an elective affinity between patriarchy and the reactionary cult of the imperial 'fatherland', there is also a similar link between feminist politics and culture and the ecologist defence of 'Mother Earth'.[1]

5. Sympathy and solidarity with the struggles of Third World people to liberate themselves from imperialist oppression, native dictatorships, hunger and misery. Although less political than the anti-imperialist movements of the 1960s, this current – today frequently composed of radicalised Christian activists – is genuinely committed to internationalist solidarity.

6. Other social movements, such as human rights organisations, movements of gays and lesbians, and Christian socialist networks, who have been establishing strong internationalist links in recent years.

An objective factor contributing to the rise of internationalist tendencies in Europe is of course the development of the European Union, which renders many old nationalist quarrels (France vs. Germany) increasingly obsolete and creates favourable conditions for common European social struggles: for instance the trade union fight for a 35-hour week. However, in the short range, the so-called 'objective economic constraints' of the international environment and in particular of the EU have been used as one of the main arguments of social-democratic governments in Europe to justify the lack of any radical social measures on the national level. The well-known socialist historian Daniel Singer answered this kind of self-legitimating discourse very accurately by pointing to the present dialectics between national and international change:

The fact that the medium sized nation-state is historically doomed in its present form does not mean that it does not

provide for the time being the first platform for social transformation. Indeed, it still provides the only possible initial
terrain. To deny it is to oppose the very idea of radical
change. The question must still first be put within national
borders even if the answers are already international,
European to begin with ... . Similarly, only a western
Europe forging a different type of society stands a chance of
preventing our future from being American. The growing
economic interdependence, the inevitability of a rapid
expansion of the movement from a national to a European
scale does not condemn individual countries, as it is being
suggested, to permanent submission to the rule of capital.
It simply condemns a socialist movement, however deep its
national roots, to internationalism.[2]

It is too soon to predict if these various ingredients will be able
to combine harmoniously and if the new internationalist
culture will unfold as a unified mass movement in Europe (or
the world). But it may be that these are the modest beginnings
of what will be the socialist internationalism of the twenty-first
century.

Notes

Introduction

1. Georges Haupt, 'Présentation', Otto Bauer, 'Remarques sur la question des nationalités' (1908), *Pluriel/Debat* no. 5, 1976, pp. 41–2. See also Claudie Weill's interesting introduction to the French edition of Bauer's book , *La question des nationalités et la social-démocratie* (Paris: EDI, 1987).
2. Bauer, *Die Nationalitätenfrage und die Sozialdemokratie* (Vienna: Wiener Volksbuchhandlung, 1924), p. xxviii; V.I. Lenin, 'The discussion on self-determination summed up' (1916), *Collected Works* (Moscow: Progress Publishers, 1960–70) vol. 22, pp. 324–5.
3. Lenin, 'Critical remarks on the national question' (1913), *Collected Works* vol. 20, p. 37; Enzo Traverso, *The Marxists and the Jewish Question: The History of a Debate, 1843–1943,* trans. Bernard Gibbons (New Jersey: Humanities Press, 1994), Ch. 5.

Chapter 1

1. Karl Marx and Friedrich Engels, 'Manifesto of the Communist Party' (1848), in Marx and Engels, *Collected Works* (New York: International Publishers, 1975–) vol. 6, pp. 502–3.
2. Engels, 'The festival of nations in London' (1845), in Marx and Engels, *Collected Works* vol. 6, p. 6. See also Marx, 'Speech on the question of free trade' (1848), in Marx and Engels, *Collected Works* vol. 6, p. 464: 'The fraternity which Free Trade would establish between the nations of the earth would not be more real, to call

cosmopolitan exploitation universal brotherhood is an idea that could only be engendered in the brain of the bourgeoisie.'

3. Marx and Engels, *The German Ideology* (1845), in Marx and Engels, *Collected Works* vol. 5, p. 73.

4. This interpretation is put forward by Roman Rosdolsky in his essay, 'Worker and fatherland: a note on a passage in *The Communist Manifesto*', *Science and Society* (London) vol. 29, no. 3 (summer 1965), p. 337.

5. Marx, 'Draft of an article on Friedrich List's book *Das nationale System der politischen Oekonomie*' (1845), in Marx and Engels, *Collected Works* vol. 4, p. 280.

6. Engels, 'The festival of nations', p. 6.

7. Ibid., p. 8.

8. Ibid., p. 3.

9. Engels, 'Louis Blanc's speech at the Dijon banquet' (1847), in Marx and Engels, *Collected Works* vol. 6, p. 411.

10. Ibid., p. 411.

11. Marx and Engels, *Collected Works* vol. 6, pp. 615–16.

12. Marx and Engels, *Selected Correspondence* (New York: International Publishers, 1942), p. 329.

13. See the passages in the prosecutor's investigations in Slansky's trial in Artur London, *On Trial* (London: Macdonald, 1970), pp 265–316.

14. (Paris: Ed. Sociales, 1950).

15. Marx and Engels, *The German Ideology*, p. 470.

16. Cogniot, *Réalité de la Nation,* p. 16. The thesis of the affinity between cosmopolitanism and nationalism was in 1950 one of the *leitmotifs* of the campaign against Tito and Rajk. For example, Cogniot writes in his work: 'The banner of cosmopolitanism drapes the bourgeois nationalism of Tito, his attempts against the security of peoples, against the independence of states, and against peace, as the Budapest trial has confirmed.' (p. 99) The thesis was to be put forward again during the Prague trials of 1952 when Slansky and his comrades were to be denounced by the prosecutor as people whose 'cosmopolitanism went hand-in-hand with Jewish nationalism.' (Cited by London, *On Trial,* p. 198.)

17. Cogniot, *Réalité de la Nation,* p. 16.

18.	Marx and Engels, *The German Ideology,* p. 51. See also p. 49: 'The prolelariat can only exist world-historically, just as communism, its activity, can only have a world-historical existence.'

19.	Marx, 'Draft of an article on Friedrich List's book', p. 281. The cosmopolitan view of Marx and Engels is still largely Euro-centred: more exactly, for them the 'centre' is less Europe as such than the industrial countries of the world: England, France, Germany, the US. On the other hand, it is clear that there also exists for Marx and Engels a *personal,* cosmopolitan dimension which shows itself in their universal cultural references, their internationalist preoccupations, their travels, etc.

20.	Bauer, *Die Nationalitätenfrage und die Sozialdemokratie* (Vienna: Wiener Volksbuchhandlung, 1924), p. 311. However, Bauer himself also underlines, in terms which are reminiscent of texts of the young Engels, the intrinsically internationalist vocation of the proletariat: 'There is no class as internally free of all national valuation in so complete a manner as the proletariat in the ascendant, a class freed of all traditions by the destructive and shattering force of capitalism, separated from the enjoyment of the national cultural possessions, in struggle against all the forces established by the historic past' (ibid., p. 153).

21.	Engels, 'Draft of a communist confession of faith' (1847), in Marx and Engels, *Collected Works* vol. 6, p. 103. The French writer Charles Andler in his celebrated commentary on the *Manifesto* names the League of the Just, Wilhelm Weitling and the English Chartists as the sources of the conception put forward by Marx and Engels on the future of nations. Charles Andler, *Introduction historique et commentaire à Marx, Engels, La Manifeste Communiste* (Paris: Société Nouvelle de Librairie et Edition, 1901), pp. 154–5.

22.	In *Manifeste Communiste* (Paris: Ed. Costes, 1953), p. 160.

23.	Solomon F. Bloom, *The World of Nations: A Study of the National Implications in the Works of Karl Marx* (New York: Columbia University Press, 1941), p. 26.

24. Bertell Ollman, 'Marx's vision of communism: a recon-
     struction', in *Critique* no. 8 (summer 1977), p. 22.
25. Ibid., p. 29. In another passage in his article Ollman
     adds, however, 'The existence of such a language does
     not mean that lesser local languages and the distinctive
     cultures which accompany them will all disappear. Latin
     and Latin culture have enriched the lives of millions long
     after the decline of the Roman empire ... .' (ibid., p. 35).
26. Marx and Engels, *The German Ideology*, p. 426.
27. Ibid., p. 394.
28. Ollman, 'Marx's vision of communism', pp. 34–5.
29. Rosdolsky, 'Worker and fatherland', p. 335.
30. Ibid., p. 337.
31. Marx, *Critique of the Gotha Programme* (New York:
     International Publishers, 1966), p. 13.
32. Marx and Engels, *Selected Correspondence*, p. 208. In an
     earlier letter to Engels (7 June 1866), Marx is more
     nuanced about the Proudhonists: he criticises their
     Franco-centrism which he describes as 'grotesque' but
     considers their agitation 'useful and explicable as a
     polemic against chauvinism' (Marx and Engels,
     Briefwechsel (Berlin: Dietz Verlag, 1953), p. 209).

Chapter 2

1. This chapter was co-written with Enzo Traverso.
2. Ephraim Nimni, 'Marx, Engels and the National
    Question', *Science and Society* vol. 53 no. 3 (1989),
    pp. 297–326.
3. Karl Marx, 'The British rule in India' (1853), in Marx
    and Engels, *Collected Works* (New York: International
    Publishers, 1975–) vol. 12, p. 132.
4. Friedrich Engels, 'Democratic Pan-Slavism' (1849), in
    Marx and Engels, *Collected Works* vol. 8, p. 365, cited in
    Horace B. Davis, *Nationalism and Socialism: Marxism
    and Labor Theories of Nationalism to 1917* (New York:
    Monthly Review Press, 1967), p. 62.
5. Engels, 'Extraordinary revelations' (1848), in Marx and
    Engels, *Collected Works* vol. 6, p. 471, cited in Réné

Gallissot, *Marxisme et Algérie* (Paris: Union Générale d'Edition, 1976), p. 25.

6. Marx, *Capital* vol. 1 (London: Lawrence and Wishart, 1974), pp. 457–8.

7. Marx, 'The future results of British rule in India' (1853), in Marx and Engels, *Collected Works* vol. 12, p. 222.

8. Engels, 'Algeria' (1857), in Marx and Engels, *Collected Works* vol. 18, p. 67, cited in Gallissot, *Marxisme et Algérie*, p. 99.

9. Marx, 'The intervention in Mexico' (1861), in Marx and Engels, *Collected Works* vol. 19, p. 71.

10. Marx, *Capital* vol. 1, p. 19.

11. Antonio Gramsci, 'The revolution against "Capital"' (1917), in *Selections from the Political Writings*, ed. Quintin Hoare, trans. John Matthews (London: Lawrence and Wishart, 1977), pp. 34–7.

12. Marx to *Otechestvenniye Zapiski* (November 1877), in Marx and Engels, *Basic Writings on Politics and Philosophy*, ed. Lewis S. Feuer (New York: Anchor Books, 1959), pp. 440–1; Marx to Zasulich (8 Mar. 1881), in *Late Marx and the Russian Road: Marx and 'the Peripheries of Capitalism'*, ed. Teodor Shanin (London: Routledge and Kegan Paul, 1984), p. 124.

13. See Chapter 3 of this book (pages 38–9), and Enzo Traverso, 'Socialismo e nazione: Rassegna di una controversia marxista', *Il Ponte* vol. 40 no. 1 (1984), p. 1.

14. See Maxime Rodinson, 'Le marxisme et la nation', *L'Homme et la société* (January–March 1968), p. 133, and Georges Haupt and Claudie Weill, 'L'eredità di Marx ed Engels e la questione nazionale', *Studi storici* vol. 15 no. 2 (1974), p. 2.

15. Marx and Engels, 'Manifesto of the Communist Party' (1848), in Marx and Engels, *Collected Works* vol. 6, p. 488.

16. See Chapter 1 of this book (pages 12–14) and Roman Rosdolsky, 'Worker and fatherland: a note on a passage in *The Communist Manifesto*', *Science and Society* (London) vol. 29, no. 3 (summer 1965), pp. 335–7.

17. Engels, 'Aus den Fragmenten zur "Geschichte Irlands"' (1870), in Marx and Engels, *Werke* (Berlin: Dietz Verlag, 1975) vol. 16, p. 499.

18. Leon Trotsky, 'The Negro question in America' (1933), in *On Black Nationalism and Self-Determination* (New York: Pathfinder, 1978), p. 28.

19. Marx to Engels (30 November 1867), in Marx and Engels, *On Colonialism* (Moscow: Foreign Languages Publishing House, n.d.), p. 323.

20. Nimni, 'Marx, Engels and the national question', pp. 308, 310.

21. Marx, 'Revolution in China and in Europe' (1863), in *Karl Marx on Colonialism and Modernization,* ed. Shlomo Avineri (New York: Anchor Books, 1969), pp. 67, 73.

22. Marx, 'History of the opium trade' (1858), in Marx and Engels, *Collected Works* vol. 16, p. 16.

23. Engels, 'Democratic Pan-Slavism' (1849), *Collected Works* vol. 8, p. 367.

24. Engels, 'The Magyar struggle' (1849), *Collected Works* vol. 8, p. 234.

25. See Michael Löwy, *Uneven and Combined Development: The Theory of Permanent Revolution* (London: Verso, 1981), p. 27.

26. Roman Rosdolsky, *Zur nationalen Frage, Friedrich Engels und das Problem der 'geschichtslosen' Völker* (Berlin: Olle and Wolter, 1979), p. 125.

27. See Georges Haupt, 'Parti-guide: le rayonnement de la social-démocratie allemande dans le Sud-Est europeen', in *L'historien et le mouvement social* (Paris: Maspéro, 1980), p. 185.

28. Otto Bauer, *Die Nationalitätenfrage und die Sozialdemokratie* (Vienna: Wiener Volksbuchhandlung, 1924), Ch. 3.

29. Rosdolsky, *Zur nationalen Frage,* pp. 116, 121.

30. See especially Claudie Weill, *L'Internationale et l'autre: Les relations inter-ethniques dans la IIe Internationale* (Paris: Arcantère, 1987).

31. See Andreu Nin, *Los movimientos de emancipación nacional* (Barcelona: Editorial Fontamara, 1977) especially pp. 70–2, and J.M. and J.L. Arenillas, *Sobre la cuestión nacional en Euskadi* (Barcelona: Editorial Fontamara, 1978).

32.   Karl Marx and Friedrich Engels, *Selected Correspondence* (Moscow: Progress Publishers, 1965), pp. 236–7.

Chapter 3

1.   Rosa Luxemburg, 'The Polish question at the international congress in London' (1896), in *The National Question,* ed. Horace B. Davis (New York: Monthly Review Press, 1976), pp. 57–8.
2.   Luxemburg, *The Industrial Development of Poland* (1898), trans. Tessa DeCarlo (New York: Campaigner Publications, 1977).
3.   V.I. Lenin, *The Development of Capitalism in Russia* (1899), in *Collected Works* (Moscow: Progress Publishers, 1960–70) vol. 3.
4.   Friedrich Engels, 'The Magyar struggle' (1849), in Marx and Engels, *Collected Works* (New York: International Publishers, 1975–) vol. 8, p. 234.
5.   Luxemburg, 'The national question and autonomy' (1908–09), in *The National Question,* pp. 115, 118.
6.   Luxemburg, 'The Junius pamphlet: the crisis in the German social democracy' (1915), in *Rosa Luxemburg Speaks,* ed. Mary-Alice Waters (New York: Pathfinder, 1970), p. 304.
7.   Luxemburg, 'Theses on the tasks of international social democracy' (1915), in *Rosa Luxemburg Speaks,* p. 329.
8.   Luxemburg, 'Sozial-patriotische Programakrobatik', in *Internazionalismus und Klassenkampf* (Neuwied: 1971).
9.   See Georg Lukács, 'Critical observations on Rosa Luxemburg's "Critique of the Russian revolution"', in *History and Class Consciousness* (London: Merlin Press, 1971), pp. 272–95.
10.   See Lenin, 'The right of nations to self-determination' (1914), *Collected Works* vol. 20, p. 430: 'It is quite understandable that in their zeal (sometimes a little excessive, perhaps) to combat the nationalistically blinded petty bourgeoisie of Poland the Polish Social Democrats should overdo things.'

11. Luxemburg, 'Foreword to the anthology *The Polish Question and the Socialist Movement*' (1905), in *The National Question,* pp. 72, 96.

12. Leon Trotsky, *The Bolsheviki and World Peace* (New York, 1918), pp. 21, 230–1, etc.

13. *Nashe Slovo* nos 130 and 135 (3 and 9 July 1915), reprinted in vol. 9 (1927) of Trotsky's *Collected Works* in Russian and in French as 'Nation et Economie' in *Pluriel-Debat* no. 4 (April 1975).

14. Joseph Stalin, 'Marxism and the national question' (1913), in *Works* (Moscow: Foreign Languages Publishing House, 1953) vol. 2, pp. 300–81.

15. Lenin, *Collected Works* vol. 35, p. 84.

16. Cf. Trotsky, *Stalin* (1940) (London: Panther History, 1969) vol. 1, p. 233.

17. Lenin, 'The right of nations to self-determination' (1914), in *Collected Works* vol. 20, p. 398.

18. Stalin, 'Marxism and the national question', pp. 306–7, 309, 305, 339.

19. Lenin, 'The national programme of the RSDLP' (1916), *Collected Works* vol. 19, p. 543, and 'Critical remarks on the national question' (1913), in *Collected Works* vol. 20, pp. 39, 50.

20. On this question, Lenin's analysis of the 1916 Rising in Ireland is a model of revolutionary realism: see 'The discussion of self-determination summed up' (1916), in *Collected Works* vol. 22, pp. 353–8.

21. Lenin, 'The socialist revolution and the right of nations to self-determination' (1916), in *Collected Works* vol. 22, p. 145.

22. Lenin, 'The discussion on self-determination', p. 344. (Translation modified.)

23. As A.S. Naïr and C. Scalabrino stressed in their excellent article, 'La question nationale dans la théorie marxiste révolutionnaire', *Partisans* no. 59–60, May–August 1971.

24. See Trotsky on African-Americans in the United States: 'An abstract criterion is not decisive in this case: much more decisive are historical consciousness, feelings and

emotions.' Trotsky, 'The Negro question in America' (1933), in *On Black Nationalism and Self-Determination* (New York: Pathfinder, 1978), p. 28.

25.   Quoted in Arthur Schlesinger Jr., *The Bitter Heritage: Vietnam and American Democracy, 1941–1966* (Boston: Houghton Mifflin, 1966), p. 108.

26.   Heinrich von Treitschke, *Politics* (London: 1916), vol. 2, p. 614.

Chapter 4

1.   Translated by Peter Drucker from 'La nation comme communauté de destin: actualité d'Otto Bauer', *Le Messager européen* no. 7 (1993).

2.   On the historical context, see Claudie Weill's remarkable book, *L'Internationale et l'autre: Les relations inter-ethniques dans la IIe Internationale* (Paris: Arcantère, 1987).

3.   Weill, 'Introduction', in Otto Bauer, *La question des nationalités et la social-démocratie* (Paris: EDI 1987), p. 9.

4.   On this topic see Enzo Traverso's brilliant work, *The Marxists and the Jewish Question: The History of a Debate, 1843–1943,* trans. Bernard Gibbons (New Jersey: Humanities Press, 1994).

5.   Bauer, *Die Nationalitätenfrage und die Sozialdemokratie* (Vienna: Wiener Volksbuchhandlung, 1924), p. 122.

6.   Bauer, *Nationalitätenfrage,* pp. 123, 129-30.

7.   Bauer, *Nationalitätenfrage,* pp. 121-2, 12–14, 6–9, 9. These three names don't refer to anyone in particular; they were just the most common Viennese Jewish names in the early twentieth century.

8.   Bauer, *Nationalitätenfrage,* p. 135.

9.   Georges Haupt, 'Les marxistes face à la question nationale: l'histoire du problème', in Haupt, Löwy and Weill, *Les marxistes et la question nationale, 1848–1914* (Paris: Maspero, 1974), p. 48. My late lamented friend Georges Haupt had grasped the importance of Bauer's contribution much better than I had at the time.

10.   Bauer, *Nationalitätenfrage,* p. 127. See on this subject Haupt's comment: 'For him a community is based on

experience inwardly lived in common by the individuals that make it up, while a society depends on "outside norms".' Haupt, 'Présentation'; Bauer, 'Remarques sur la question des nationalités' (1908), in *Pluriel* no. 5, 1976, p. 44.

11. Bauer, *Nationalitätenfrage*, p. 127–8.
12. Bauer, *Nationalitätenfrage*, p. 133.
13. See Benedict Anderson's book *Imagined Communities: Reflections on the Origin and Spread of Nationalism* (London: Verso, 1983), as well as Eric Hobsbawm's work *Nations and Nationalism since 1780: Programme, Myth, Reality* (Cambridge: Cambridge University Press, 1990).
14. Bauer, *Nationalitätenfrage*, pp. 145–8, 118.
15. Bauer, *Nationalitätenfrage*, p. xxviii.

Chapter 5

1. Hans Kohn, *Nationalism* (Princeton: Von Nostrand, 1955), p. 9.
2. Ibid., p. 15.
3. Tom Nairn, 'The Modern Janus', *New Left Review* no. 94 (November–December 1975), p. 15.
4. Karl Marx, 'Draft of an article on Friedrich List's book *Das nationale System der politischen Oekonomie*' (1845), in Marx and Engels, *Collected Works* (New York: International Publishers, 1975–) vol. 4, p. 280. See also Chapter 1 [page 7].
5. Leon Trotsky, 'Introduction to the German edition' (1930), *The Permanent Revolution* and *Results and Prospects* (New York: Pathfinder Press, 1969), p. 150.
6. Karl Kautsky, 'Die moderne Nationalität', *Die Neue Zeit* vol. V (1887), p. 451.
7. Trotsky, 'Nation et Economie' (1915), in *Pluriel-Debat* no. 4 (April 1975), p. 48. This analysis is borrowed from Enzo Traverso's excellent paper 'Socialismo e nazione: rasssegna di una controversia marxista', *Il Ponte* vol. 40, no. 1 (1984), p. 60.
8. Vladimir Medem, *The National Question and Social Democracy* (Vilna, 1906), quoted in Arieh Yaari, *Le défi*

national: Les théories marxistes sur la question nationale à l'épreuve de l'histoire (Paris: Anthropos, 1978), pp. 186–7.

9. Traverso, 'Socialismo e nazione', p. 61.

Chapter 6

1. Theodor Adorno, *Modèles critiques* (Paris: Payot, 1964), p. 106.
2. Hannah Arendt, *The Burden of Our Time* (London: Secker and Warburg, 1951), p. 267.
3. Rosa Luxemburg, 'Fragment über Krieg, nationale Frage und Revolution', in *Die Russische Revolution* (Frankfurt: Europäische Verlagsanstalt, 1963), p. 82.
4. On this see the remarkable essay by Catherine Samary, *The Fragmentation of Yugoslavia* (Amsterdam: IIRE Notebook for Study and Research no. 19/20, 1992).
5. Quoted by Eric Hobsbawm in 'The perils of the new nationalism', *The Nation* (November 1991), p. 556.
6. Trotsky, 'The Negro question in America' (1933), in *On Black Nationalism and Self-Determination* (New York: Pathfinder, 1978), p. 28.
7. Eric Hobsbawm, *Nations and Nationalism since 1780: Programme, Myth, Reality* (Cambridge: Cambridge University Press, 1990), pp. 163, 170, 181.
8. Ernst Gellner, 'Nationalism and politics in Eastern Europe', *New Left Review* no. 189 (October 1991), p. 131.
9. For an interesting and provocative analysis of this new upsurge of the national minorities against the established nation-states, and its anti-capitalist potential, one should see the recent work of a Basque Marxist: Gurutz Jauregui Bereciartu, *Contra el Estado-nación: En torno al hecho y la cuestión nacional* (Madrid: Siglo XXI, 1986).
10. *Bild am Sontag* (26 January 1992).
11. Adorno, *Modèles critiques,* p. 106.
12. I am referring more extensively to Latin America because I am more familiar with this area of the Third World.

13. 'Declaración de São Paulo', *Inprecor para América Latina* no. 6 (July 1990), pp. 5–6.
14. Hobsbawm, *Nations and Nationalism,* p. 133.

Chapter 7

1. By the way, *Mother Earth* was the name of an internationalist journal founded in the US before the First World War by the well-known anarchist leader Emma Goldman.
2. Daniel Singer, 'Radical change and Europe's nation state', paper presented at the 1987 Cavtat Conference (Yugoslavia) on Socialism, Nations, International Cooperation, p. 10.

Bibliography

Adorno, Theodor *Modèles critiques* (Paris: Payot, 1964).

Anderson, Benedict *Imagined Communities: Reflections on the Origin and Spread of Nationalism* (London: Verso, 1983).

Andler, Charles *Introduction historique et commentaire à Marx, Engels, La Manifeste Communiste* (Paris: Société Nouvelle de Librairie et Edition, 1901).

Arendt, Hannah *The Burden of Our Time* (London: Secker and Warburg, 1951).

Arenillas, J.M. and J.L. *Sobre la cuestión nacional en Euskadi* (Barcelona: Editorial Fontamara, 1978).

Bauer, Otto *Die Nationalitätenfrage und die Sozialdemokratie* (Vienna: Wiener Volksbuchhandlung, 1924).

Bereciartu, Gurutz Jauregui *Contra el Estado-nación: En torno al hecho y la cuestión nacional* (Madrid: Siglo XXI, 1986).

Bloom, Solomon F. *The World of Nations: A Study of the National Implications in the Works of Karl Marx* (New York: Columbia University Press, 1941).

Cogniot, Georges *Réalité de la Nation: L'attrape-nigaud du cosmopolitisme* (Paris: Ed. Sociales, 1950).

Davis, Horace B. *Nationalism and Socialism: Marxism and Labor Theories of Nationalism to 1917* (New York: Monthly Review Press, 1967).

Engels, Friedrich 'Algeria' (1857), in Marx and Engels, *Collected Works* (New York: International Publishers, 1975) vol. 18.

—— 'Aus den Fragmenten zur "Geschichte Irlands"' (1870), in Marx and Engels, *Werke* (Berlin: Dietz Verlag, 1975) vol. 16.

—— 'Democratic Pan-Slavism' (1849), in Marx and Engels, *Collected Works* vol. 8.

—— 'Draft of a communist confession of faith' (1847), in Marx and Engels, *Collected Works* vol. 6.

—— 'Extraordinary revelations' (1848), in Marx and Engels, *Collected Works* vol. 6.

—— 'The festival of nations in London' (1845), in Marx and Engels, *Collected Works* vol. 6.

—— 'Louis Blanc's speech at the Dijon banquet' (1847), in Marx and Engels, *Collected Works* vol. 6.

—— 'The Magyar struggle' (1849), in Marx and Engels, *Collected Works* vol. 8.

Gallissot, Réné *Marxisme et Algérie* (Paris: Union Générale d'Edition, 1976).

Gellner, Ernst 'Nationalism and politics in Eastern Europe', *New Left Review* no. 189 (October 1991).

Haupt, Georges 'Les marxistes face à la question nationale: l'histoire du problème', in Haupt, Löwy and Weill, *Les marxistes et la question nationale, 1848–1914* (Paris: Maspero, 1974).

—— 'Parti-guide: le rayonnement de la social-démocratie allemande dans le Sud-Est europeen', in *L'historien et le mouvement social* (Paris: Maspéro, 1980).

—— 'Présentation', Otto Bauer, 'Remarques sur la question des nationalités' (1908), *Pluriel/Debat* no. 5, 1976.

Haupt, Georges and Claudie Weill 'L'eredità di Marx ed Engels e la questione nazionale', *Studi storici* vol. 15 no. 2 (1974).

Hobsbawm, Eric *Nations and Nationalism since 1780: Programme, Myth, Reality* (Cambridge: Cambridge University Press, 1990).

—— 'The perils of the new nationalism', *The Nation* (November 1991).

Kautsky, Karl 'Die moderne Nationalität', *Die Neue Zeit* vol. V (1887).

Kohn, Hans *Nationalism* (Princeton: Von Nostrand, 1955).

Lenin, V.I. 'Critical remarks on the national question' (1913), in *Collected Works* vol. 20 (Moscow: Progress Publishers, 1960–70).

—— *The Development of Capitalism in Russia* (1899), in *Collected Works* vol. 3.

—— 'The discussion on self-determination summed up' (1916), in *Collected Works* vol. 22.

—— 'The national programme of the RSDLP' (1913), in *Collected Works* vol. 19.

—— 'The right of nations to self-determination' (1914), in *Collected Works* vol. 20.

—— 'The socialist revolution and the right of nations to self-determination' (1916), in *Collected Works* vol. 22.

Löwy, Michael *Uneven and Combined Development: The Theory of Permanent Revolution* (London: Verso, 1981).

Lukács, Georg 'Critical observations on Rosa Luxemburg's "Critique of the Russian revolution"', in *History and Class Consciousness* (London: Merlin Press, 1971).

Luxemburg, Rosa 'Foreword to the anthology *The Polish Question and the Socialist Movement*' (1905), in *The National Question,* ed. Horace B. Davis (New York: Monthly Review Press, 1976).

—— 'Fragment über Krieg, nationale Frage und Revolution', in *Die Russische Revolution* (Frankfurt: Europäische Verlagsanstalt, 1963).

—— *The Industrial Development of Poland* (1898), trans. Tessa DeCarlo (New York: Campaigner Publications, 1977).

—— 'The Junius pamphlet: the crisis in the German social democracy' (1915), in *Rosa Luxemburg Speaks,* ed. Mary-Alice Waters (New York: Pathfinder, 1970).

—— 'The national question and autonomy' (1908–09), in *The National Question.*

—— 'The Polish question at the international congress in London' (1896), in *The National Question.*

—— 'Sozial-patriotische Programakrobatik', in *Internazional-ismus und Klassenkampf* (Neuwied: 1971).

Marx, Karl 'The British rule in India' (1853), in Marx and Engels, *Collected Works* (New York: International Publishers, 1975) vol. 12.

—— *Capital* vol. 1 (1867) (London: Lawrence and Wishart, 1974).

—— *Critique of the Gotha Programme* (1875) (New York: International Publishers, 1966).

—— 'Draft of an article on Friedrich List's book *Das nationale System der politischen Oekonomie*' (1845), in Marx and Engels, *Collected Works* vol. 4.

—— 'The future results of British rule in India' (1853), in Marx and Engels, *Collected Works* vol. 12.

—— 'History of the opium trade' (1858), in Marx and Engels, *Collected Works* vol. 16.

—— 'The intervention in Mexico' (1861), in Marx and Engels, *Collected Works* vol. 19.

——'Revolution in China and in Europe' (1863), in *Karl Marx on Colonialism and Modernization,* ed. Shlomo Avineri (New York: Anchor Books, 1969).

—— 'Speech on the question of free trade' (1848), in Marx and Engels, *Collected Works* vol. 6.

Marx, Karl and Friedrich Engels *The German Ideology* (1845), in Marx and Engels, *Collected Works* vol. 5.

—— 'Manifesto of the Communist Party' (1848), in Marx and Engels, *Collected Works* vol. 6.

—— *Selected Correspondence* (New York: International Publishers, 1942); also (Moscow: Progress Publishers, 1965).

Naïr, A.S. and C. Scalabrino 'La question nationale dans la théorie marxiste révolutionnaire', *Partisans* no. 59–60, May–Aug. 1971.

Nairn, Tom 'The Modern Janus', *New Left Review* no. 94 (November–December 1975).

Nimni, Ephraim 'Marx, Engels and the National Question', *Science and Society* vol. 53 no. 3 (1989).

Nin, Andreu *Los movimientos de emancipación nacional* (Barcelona: Editorial Fontamara, 1977).

Ollman, Bertell 'Marx's vision of communism: a reconstruction', in *Critique* no. 8 (summer 1977).

Rodinson, Maxime 'Le marxisme et la nation', *L'Homme et la société* (January– March 1968).

Rosdolsky, Roman 'Worker and fatherland: a note on a passage in *The Communist Manifesto*', *Science and Society* (London) vol. 29 no. 3 (summer 1965).

—— *Zur nationalen Frage, Friedrich Engels und das Problem der 'geschichtslosen' Völker* (Berlin: Olle and Wolter, 1979).

Samary, Catherine *The Fragmentation of Yugoslavia* (Amsterdam: IIRE Notebook for Study and Research no. 19/20,1992).

Shanin, Teodor (ed.) *Late Marx and the Russian Road: Marx and the 'Peripheries of Capitalism'* (London: Routledge and Kegan Paul, 1984).

Singer, Daniel 'Radical change and Europe's nation state', paper presented at the 1987 Cavtat Conference (Yugoslavia) on Socialism, Nations, International Cooperation.

Stalin, Joseph 'Marxism and the national question', in *Works* (Moscow: Foreign Languages Publishing House, 1953) vol. 2.

Traverso, Enzo *The Marxists and the Jewish Question: The History of a Debate, 1843–1943,* trans. Bernard Gibbons (New Jersey: Humanities Press, 1994).

——'Socialismo e nazione: Rassegna di una controversia marxista', *Il Ponte* vol. 40 no. 1 (1984).

Trotsky Leon, *The Bolsheviki and World Peace* (New York: 1918).

—— 'Introduction to the German edition' (1930), *The Permanent Revolution* and *Results and Prospects* (New York: Pathfinder Press, 1969).

—— 'Nation et Economie' (1915), in *Pluriel-Debat* no. 4 (April 1975).

—— 'The Negro question in America' (1933), in *On Black Nationalism and Self-Determination* (New York: Pathfinder, 1978).

—— *Stalin* (1940) (London: Panther History, 1969).

Weill, Claudie *L'Internationale et l'autre: Les relations inter-ethniques dans la IIe Internationale* (Paris: Arcantère, 1987).

—— 'Introduction', Otto Bauer, *La question des nationalités et la social-démocratie* (Paris: EDI, 1987).

Yaari, Arieh *Le défi national: Les théories marxistes sur la question nationale à l'épreuve de l'histoire* (Paris: Anthropos, 1978).

Index